MILTON TO OUIDA

Milton to Ouida

A Collection of Essays

by

BONAMY DOBRÉE

NEW YORK

BARNES & NOBLE, INC.

Publishers · Booksellers · Since 1873

First published in 1970 by
FRANK CASS AND COMPANY LIMITED
67 Great Russell Street, London WC1

First published in the United States, 1970
by Barnes & Noble, Inc.

SBN 389 01124 x

Printed in Great Britain

CONTENTS

MILTON AND DRYDEN

A Comparison in
Poetic Ideas and Poetic Method*

IT would be hard, I imagine, to name two great poets living at the same time, who were in most ways so markedly different as Milton and Dryden are, in scope, in intent, in handling of the medium. Yet they present certain likenesses; they are subject in common to certain limitations; both had at their disposal, and used, a mass of material which we do not find much used, if at all, by other poets of their day. And if these likenesses, perhaps these limitations, are partly due, as one would expect, to their having lived in the same age, that is not the whole story.

The age they lived in was not, of course, quite the same. Milton was older than Dryden: he was born in 1608, whereas Dryden was not born until 1631, and Milton was an acknowledged poet while Dryden was still in the cradle. Yet both underwent what was apparently a very important poetic influence in their adolescent years, an influence which they both had to break away from—namely, Sylvester's translation of Du Bartas, the *Divine Weekes and Workes*. To us this is an infinitely dreary fabrication; its matter and its manner are both repugnant to us; it is turgid, violent, overloaded—and it is intolerably long. We can easily see, however, why it might attract two young poets, both determined to do great things, and

* Lecture before the Tudor and Stuart Club, December 11, 1935. Reprinted from E.L.H., *A Journal of English Literary History*, Vol. 3, no. 1, March, 1936.

both weary of the far more stiff matter, intellectually and structurally, offered them by the poets whom, since Dr. Johnson's day, we have called the Metaphysicals. It is an enormous pseudo-epic, read by both when the epic, as an idea at least, was coming into fashion; it was the 'noblest' form of poetry, and so it would appeal to two ambitious young poets. It appeared also to embody the scientific ideas of the day, the New Learning, which would be an added satisfaction. No doubt the appeal for Milton was especially in its being a poem on the Creation written by a Protestant poet; it dealt with the relation of God to man; equally characteristic is that what appealed to Dryden was not the subject-matter, but the style. Sylvester seemed to him to have hit upon a good way of writing poetry. 'When I was a Boy,' he came to confess in the Dedication of *The Spanish Fryar*, 'I thought inimitable *Spenser* a mean Poet in comparison of *Sylvester's Dubartas*: and was rapt into an ecstasie when I read these lines:

> Now, when the Winter's keener breath began
> To Chrystallize the Baltick Ocean;
> To glaze the Lakes, to bridle up the Floods,
> And periwig with Snow the bald-pate Woods:

I am much deceiv'd,' he added, in the disillusion and wisdom of riper years, 'if this be not abominable fustian.' It is not without significance that the greatest work of both poets was to be religious poetry, but the difference in their attitude towards the poem is of equal significance. Milton was interested in the matter, the vastness of the conception—though indeed the metrical versions of the psalms he wrote as a boy of fifteen show more than traces of Sylvester's style; whereas Dryden was interested in the method, the craft. To Milton the craft was only a means, to Dryden, it was, partly at least, an end.

But though they reacted, as they were bound to react, against metaphysical poetry, it was not without its influence on their work, and to clarify this side of their writings I may perhaps be permitted to run over a few commonplaces with regard to this form of poetry. My excuse must be there was latterly, in our own day, a strong revival of interest in the metaphysical poets—now a trifle abated; and it is worth noticing that the points of attraction were three: the subject-matter, the conceits, and the diction.

The interest in the subject-matter arose, I think, from a certain similarity of Jacobean times with our own. During Donne's life the educated world was much moved by the New Learning (which made Du Bartas' poem popular), by the beginnings of the scientific approach as best expressed in Bacon's writing; mediaevalism, with its old assumptions, was being broken down. In our day, too, many assumptions collapsed, the romantic ones we might say (to class them generally), undermined by what we can in our own turn call the New Learning, especially ethnology and psycho-analysis. I need not expatiate on the effect of either of these re-orientations of thought; but I would like to suggest that in both periods the minds of men, and especially of poets, were turned in upon their inner reactions, their own responses to emotions and ideas, especially to their emotions with respect to ideas. Metaphysical poetry, as you will remember, has been aptly described as embodying the emotional apprehension of thought: the thought is not produced as an expression of the emotion, but is itself the emotion to be expressed. But by the time Milton, and more so Dryden, came to their maturity, that attitude towards self as a curious instrument to be investigated had died down. How much through a natural process, since thought, and indeed the attitude towards life is to some extent a matter of fashion—or, to give it a more grandiose name, the climate of thought—and how much because the Civil War and all that preceded and followed it turned men's minds outward, it is impossible to say. But the fact remains that Dryden is the most impersonal of our poets; and that Milton, though a sublime egotist, perhaps because he was so ingenuous an egotist, took his thoughts and feelings for granted. In them, therefore, the commanding poets of their age, metaphysical emotion—using metaphysical in this context only—had no place. 'It is interesting to speculate', Mr. Eliot remarks, 'whether it is not a misfortune that two of the greatest masters of diction in our language, Milton and Dryden, triumphed with a disregard of the soul.' It is true that though the soul figures a good deal in their poetry, you never find them exploring it.

When we come to conceits, we are on more doubtful ground. We have first to reach a distinction between the metaphysical conceit and the conceit ordinary. The line is difficult to draw in practice, but in theory, perhaps, it is something as follows. The ordinary conceit is a flowery image, or metaphor: it illustrates or expands what is being said, or is a decoration drawn from the winds of fancy. A typical one might be this from a sonnet of Spenser:

> When my abodes prefixed time is spent,
> My cruell fayre streight bids me wend my way:
> but then fro heauen most hideous stormes are sent
> as willing me against her will to stay.

That is obvious and easy, and will offend no one. A storm may, most opportunely, prevent your leaving the house of your beloved; you may easily regard it as providential; from there it is only a step to believe, or at any rate to say, that it was especially sent. But the metaphysical conceit involves thought, what used to be called wit, that is, the unexpected bringing together of ideas that seem to have nothing in common. Let me take a fairly simple one from Marvell:

> As Lines so Loves *oblique* may well
> Themselves in every Angle greet:
> But ours so truly *Paralel*,
> Though infinite can never meet.

The conceit is itself the idea; it is the intellectual clash that strikes the emotional spark; without the conceit the verses have no point. It does not illustrate, it illuminates. When you grasp the conceit you have the idea of the poem; if you do not grasp it, you are lost.

Both Milton and Dryden, it must frankly be admitted, attempted the metaphysical conceit without having, in this sense, the metaphysical equipment. It was not in the intellectual climate of their age (Marvell is a survival), and they are standing examples that you can be a good, I should say a great poet, and yet be a bad metaphysical one. Let us take Dryden first, as the worst offender. In his poem on the death from small-pox of Lord Hastings, he described the horrible symptoms as follows:

> Blisters with pride swell'd, which th'row's flesh did sprout
> Like Rose-buds, stuck i' th' Lilly-skin about.
> Each little Pimple had a Tear in it,
> To wail the fault its rising did commit:

No comment is called for; but it is only fair to remember that Dryden was a schoolboy when he perpetrated that horrible farrago, and that he later represented his 'Clevelandisms' as he called them: yet he did not free himself of the strained conceit until after, some years later, he had written *Annus Mirabilis.*

Milton also erred, but not so excruciatingly. Still, when we look at the Nativity Ode, written when he was twenty-one, we may feel that he blundered heavily more than once, especially in

> So when the Sun in bed,
> Curtain'd with cloudy red,
> Pillows his chin upon an Orient wave,

a conception only saved from utter ridiculousness by the swing and music of the last line, if then. Professor Grierson, however, considers that Milton's conceits were of the school of Spenser and Crashaw, rather than of Donne's, and quotes a stanza of *The Passion*, a poem of a year later, to make his point. But we can take another stanza, which he does not quote:

> Or should I thence hurried on viewles wing,
> Take up a weeping on the Mountains wilde,
> The gentle neighbourhood of grove and spring
> Would soon unboosom all their Echoes milde,
> And I (for grief is easily beguild)
>   Might think th'infection of my sorrows loud,
> Had got a race of mourners on som pregnant cloud.

That is not very happy; and perhaps it is not altogether to be regretted that at this point Milton abandoned the poem as being on a subject above his years. His is hardly the same sort of conceit as the Spenserian one of the providential cloud. But even supposing he was trying to use the conceit as the Italians and Crashaw used it, let us see how he does it. In the last stanza but one of *The Passion* he imagines himself weeping at 'that sad Sepulchral rock', Christ's tomb:

> Yet on the softned Quarry would I score
> My plaining vers as lively as before;
>   For sure so well instructed are my tears,
> That they would fitly fall in order'd Characters.

Would they? we wonder. And now to Crashaw *Upon the Death of a Gentleman:*

> Eyes are vocal, tears have tongues,
> And there be words not made with lungs;—
> Sententious showers! O, let them fall,
> Their cadence is rhetorical.

That is completely rounded, self-sufficing, and very far from the kind of thing Milton was attempting. This is not to deny that, as he said, Spenser was his master, in the main: but it is fairly clear that he did try to imitate the metaphysicals, and I agree with Mr. Tillyard in supposing that when Milton abjured 'our late fantastics' he meant Giles and Phineas Fletcher, and not, as Dr. Grierson holds, all the metaphysical school. Milton, moreover, did write one poem in their true manner, in which the conceit is the poem; I do not mean either of the ponderously jesting poems on Hobson, but the one on Shakespeare prefixed to the Second Folio, and written in 1630.

> What needs my *Shakespear* for his honour'd Bones,
> The labour of an age in piled Stones,
> Or that his hallow'd reliques should be hid
> Under a Star-ypointing *Pyramid*?
> Dear son of memory, great heir of Fame,
> What need'st thou such weak witnes of thy name?
> Thou in our wonder and astonishment
> Hast built thy self a live-long Monument.
> For whilst to th'shame of slow-endeavouring art,
> Thy easie numbers flow, and that each part
> Hath from the leaves of thy unvalu'd Book,
> Those Delphick lines with deep impression took,
> Then thou our fancy of it self bereaving,
> Dost make us Marble with too much conceaving;
> And so Sepulcher'd in such pomp dost lie.
> That Kings for such a Tomb would wish to die.

Though Shakespeare requires no pyramid of actual stone, a marble pyramid is indeed formed by our wonder and astonishment; each part of us, each faculty, has taken the impression of his writings, so that our fancy is obliterated; and since we have no fancy left, we are turned to marble. It is significant that in the 1645 edition, in the line

> Thy easie numbers flow, and that each part

the word 'part' is changed to 'heart,' breaking the conceit in two, and depriving the poem of half its 'metaphysical' structure.

Milton and Dryden were alike then in this, that they rejected the metaphysical conceit; indeed it suited the temper of neither of their minds. Remains then the diction, and here we come to an evident divergence. The great virtue of the metaphysicals was their homely language, their attempt to be direct in speech; their diction was simple and sensuous; their phrasing was natural, and had an unconventional purity. For them, as for Wordsworth, but not, intermediately, for Gray, the

language of the age was also to be the language of poetry:
they acknowledged no especially 'poetic' words. The difference
between Milton and Dryden is that the first, whatever he may
have declared, went back on this ever-rediscovered tradition,
and built up a diction of his own, while Dryden used and developed the tradition. Milton made the language stiff and
tortuous, even distorted, unusable in that form by other
poets, as Keats was to discover, but Dryden made it miraculously flexible. Milton may be the greater poet of the two, but
in this respect he injured our poetry, while Dryden conferred
upon it the greatest possible benefit. How differently the two
poets came to use the language can be seen when we compare
them working at the same sort of thing in the fullness of their
respective powers. Let me first take Dalila appealing to Samson, and then Cleopatra appealing to Antony. This is Dalila:

> Yet hear me *Samson;* not that I endeavour
> To lessen or extenuate my offence,
> But that on th'other side if it be weigh'd
> By it self, with aggravations not surcharg'd,
> Or else with just allowance counterpois'd
> I may, if possible, thy pardon find
> The easier towards me, or thy hatred less.
> First, granting, as I do, it was a weakness
> In me, but incident to all our sex,
> Curiosity, inquisitive, importune
> Of secrets, then with like infirmity
> To publish them, both common female faults:
> Was it not weakness also to make known
> For importunity, that is for naught,
> Wherein consisted all thy strength and safety?

And now Cleopatra:

> How shall I plead my cause when you, my Judge
> Already have condemn'd me? Shall I bring
> The Love you bore me for my Advocate?
> That now is turn'd against me, that destroys me;
> For love, once past, is, at the best forgotten;

> But oftner sours to hate: 'twill please my Lord
> To ruine me, and therefore I'll be guilty.
> But, could I once have thought it would have pleas'd you,
> That you would pry, with narrow searching eyes
> Into my faults, severe to my destruction,
> And watching all advantages with care
> That serve to make me wretched? Speak, my Lord
> For I end here. Though I deserve this usage
> Was it like you to give it?

That is as complicated a passage as Dryden ever wrote; yet how lucid, how flexible it is compared with Milton's. How comely it is, and how reviving, to the spirits of weak men long oppressed with the strain of following Milton! It reveals more, however, than the evident fact that Milton's style was not suitable for drama: it shows that Milton in his poetry was trying to do something quite different from what Dryden aimed at.

The difference in approach, in aim, in method, could be seen perhaps more clearly in poems, again of like kind, written when each poet was comparatively young, if we could find them: we have indeed two funerary poems which it is extremely useful to compare, but Dryden was further advanced when he wrote his *To the Memory of Mr. Oldham*, than Milton was when he wrote his *Epitaph on the Marchioness of Winchester*. Yet, it is as well to take Milton when he was still under the Shakespearean and Spenserian influences, traces of which it is harder to find in his later work, for this earlier stage shows certain aspects of his poetry which, though always there, became obscured. I will take only four lines from Milton, though they form part of a long sentence:

> But the fair blossom hangs the head
> Sideways as on a dying bed,
> And those Pearls of dew she wears,
> Prove to be presaging tears. . . .

They make us think at once of the sort of verse later to be

written by his friend and associate Marvell, not merely because
of the inevitable reminder of the *Horatian Ode*, with its

> But bow'd his comely Head,
> Down as upon a Bed.

but because of the general feeling of the verse, which you get
too from the *Fawn*, or almost any poem of Marvell's, a feeling
of graciousness, a sense of grace, you might almost say. It is
not rare in the early Milton, in *Arcades*, for instance, the fore-
shadow of *Comus*, in some ways so markedly Shakespearean.
Milton here is relying upon mellifluousness, and sensual and
verbal association: he is creating atmosphere. Now take Dryden on Oldham, justly famous as a thing perfect in its kind:

> Farewell, too little and too lately known,
> Whom I began to think and call my own:
> For sure our Souls were near alli'd, and thine
> Cast in the same poetick mold with mine.
> One common Note on either Lyre did strike,
> And Knaves and Fools we both abhorr'd alike.
> To the same goal did both our Studies drive:
> The last set out the soonest did arrive.
> Thus *Nisus* fell upon the slippery place,
> Whilst his young Friend perform'd and won the Race.
> O early ripe! to thy abundant Store
> What could advancing Age have added more?
> It might (what Nature never gives the Young)
> Have taught the Numbers of thy Native Tongue.
> But Satire needs not those, and Wit will shine
> Through the harsh Cadence of a rugged Line.
> A noble Error, and but seldom made,
> When Poets are by too much force betray'd.
> Thy gen'rous Fruits, though gather'd ere their prime,
> Still shew'd a Quickness; and maturing Time
> But mellows what we write to the dull Sweets of Rhyme.
> Once more, hail and farewell! Farewell thou young,
> But ah! too short, *Marcellus* of our Tongue!
> Thy Brows with Ivy and with Laurels bound;
> But Fate and gloomy night encompass thee around.

That is almost dry in tone: it is a mass of *clichés*, of well-worn literary allusions: it owes nothing to verbal, as opposed to intellectual, association. It relies for its effect entirely on the thing stated, and the sincerity with which it is stated: no more emotion is to be aroused than the occasion calls for. Statement and balance, not atmosphere, are the things upon which Dryden is intent to build his poetry—and 'numbers', of which more immediately.

Seeking still for likenesses, which will again lead to a difference, we find that Milton and Dryden both thought they had a mission. Milton's sense of a mission was, one might almost say, innate; Dryden's was self-imposed. Dryden's, moreover, was impersonal: his business was, not so much to be a great poet himself, but to reform our numbers, our prosody, and indeed our language. Milton's duty, on the other hand, was to write a great poem, a task that might in itself be impersonal, but which, as he saw it, involved making himself into a great poet; and this meant first building up in himself the pattern of a great and good man. He felt himself dedicated. This was, of course, a part of that intense egotism, which served him in such very good stead. I need not here resort to the relevant passages, nor laboriously reveal how *Lycidas* is not a lament upon Edward King but a poem about John Milton; yet it is significant that Milton nearly always, directly or indirectly, speaks about himself, whereas Dryden very rarely does so: here and there in a prologue or epilogue, or in a preface, and once in *Religio Laici*, but that is nearly all. These things are well known; but I would like to draw from them a deduction which though fairly easy to draw may possibly be suggestive, and has not, I think, been developed to any extent in discussing the two poets. It is that Milton, in a sense, was incapable of treating an abstract idea and turning it into great poetry: no idea could set the poetic faculties at work within him unless it was one that affected him profoundly as an individual. There are bad lines in *Paradise Lost* where he talks of war, or again where he

B

discusses the digestive processes of the angels, where they

> Tasting concoct, digest, assimilate,
> And corporeal to incorporeal turn.

For Milton it was certainly true that emotion had to be the material for thought: Dryden could appropriate a thought direct.

Such statements are dangerously vague, and are best clarified, though not, I fear, substantiated, by illustration. Let me take passages where each treats of the same thing, namely the conception of God as light. I cannot here, of course, go into the fascinating question of Milton's religious beliefs, his Mortalist heresies, his cabbalistic leanings; but the conception of God as light is not confined to esoteric sects, and it was shared to some extent by Dryden. Milton, because of his blindness, however, had occasion to know, to feel as deeply as a human being can feel, what a divine thing light is. Two passages stand out: Samson's opening soliloquy, and the invocation to light in *Paradise Lost*. Samson, you will remember, is fairly explicit as to light being God, at least as to light being that part of God that is in the soul. 'O first created Beam,' is how he addresses God, followed by

> and thou great Word
> Let there be light, and light was over all.

He goes on:

> Since light so necessary is to life,
> And almost life itself, if it be true
> That light is in the Soul,
> She all in every part. . . .

In *Paradise Lost* (Book 3) we get, as you know, the clearest exposition.

> Hail holy light, ofspring of Heav'n first-born,
> Or of th' Eternal Coeternal beam

> May I express thee unblam'd? since God is light,
> And never but in unapproached light
> Dwelt from Eternitie, dwelt then in thee,
> Bright effluence of bright essence increate.

None of that is verbiage, nor mere poetic imagery. Whenever Milton touches upon light he is profoundly moved: he *knows* that God is light, for his own experience has taught him so. Dryden, by what cross-current of thought in seventeenth-century philosophy it might be worth while to explore, also believes that God is light, so dazzlingly that man can never see him. In *The Hind and the Panther* he declares

> Thy throne is darkness in th' abyss of light,
> A blaze of glory that forbids the sight.

He was indeed fond of 'the abyss of light', and we have it again in that strange religious play, *Tyrannick Love*, where Damilcar, a half-spirit, addresses Amariel, St. Catherine's guardian angel:

> Mercy, bright Spirit, I already feel
> The piercing edge of thy immortal steel:
> Thou Prince of day, from Elements Art free;
> And I all body when compar'd to thee.
> Thou tread'st th'Abyss of light!
> And where it streams with open eyes canst go:
> We wander in the Fields of Earth below:
> Changelings and Fooles of Heav'n; and thence shut out,
> Wildly we roam in discontent about:
> Gross-heavy-fed, next man in ignorance and sin,
> And spotted all without; and dusky all within.
> Without thy Sword I perish by thy sight,
> I reel, I stagger, and am drunk with light.

That is a fine glowing passage, in the best Dryden manner: the idea does not remain cold; but it is, we are conscious, the exposition of an intellectual idea; it is not felt in the bones as Milton felt it. But then, and here is another consequence of Milton's egotism and Dryden's impersonality, whereas Milton

believed by direct experience, *through* faith, Dryden thought
that such knowledge was beyond human grasp, and had to be
accepted *on* faith. Milton, his grapplings witness it, was in-
eradicably Protestant; Dryden, through a simpler acceptance,
was compelled ultimately to become Catholic. I must not be
thought to be commenting on the respective characters of the
Churches: I am, emphatically, not saying that Catholicism is
simpler than Protestantism: all I am endeavouring to do is to
comment on the position of two particular men.

But in the result, for Milton, as a Protestant, everything had
to pass the test of thought, had to be born of emotion strong
enough to give birth to thought. For reason with him is the
divine attribute in man, though indeed it is a humanly ratiocinative faculty, and not intuitive as it is in the angels. Again
and again he insists on reason. Thus Michael tells Adam, that
since the original lapse

> true Libertie
> Is lost, which always with right Reason dwells
> Twinn'd, and from her hath no dividual being:
> Reason in man obscur'd, or not obeyed,
> Immediately inordinate desires
> And upstart Passions catch the Government
> From Reason, and to servitude reduce
> Man till then free:

Again, speaking of wedded love:

> love refines
> The thoughts, and heart enlarges, hath his seat
> In Reason,

and again, it is 'founded in *Reason*'. Reason, then, is the highest
faculty in man: it is to that which, in the end, Milton always
appeals. Dryden, on the other hand, was dubious of reason: he
shared the scepticism which proved such fertile soil for the
Roman Catholic proselytisers, a scepticism which ran through
the century, perhaps as part of the New Learning, but to some

extent, certainly, through the reading of the *Apologie de Rai-mond Sebond*, an influence patent from the very beginning of the century in Shakespeare, to the very end of it in Halifax. Take the opening lines of *Religio Laici*, where Dryden belittles reason and aggrandises faith:

> Dim, as the borrow'd beams of Moon and Stars
> To *lonely, weary, wand'ring* Travellers
> Is Reason to the *Soul:* And as on high
> Those rowling Fires *discover* but the Sky
> Not light us *here;* so *Reason's* glimmering Ray
> Was lent, not to *assure* our *doubtfull* way,
> But *guide* up upward to a *better Day,*
> And as those nightly Tapers disappear
> When Day's bright Lord ascends our Hemisphere;
> So pale grows *Reason* at *Religion's* sight;
> So *dyes,* and so *dissolves* in *Supernatural Light.*

More than once we find Dryden asking 'How can finite measure infinite?' The question would have shocked Milton, for whom reason was part of the universal light which was God. Dryden, on the other hand, once he was securely con-verted, was full of scorn for 'private reason'.

Yet it is more than a little curious to find that, on any point of real difficulty, Milton, while exalting reason, is careful never to appeal to it; and that Dryden, always sceptical of what the mind can do, is the greatest ratiocinative poet in the language. It is true that he argues on orthodox lines: he has merged his private reason into that of the Church. There is indeed a mov-ing note in one of his rare personal references, this in *The Hind and the Panther*, where he deplores his early upbringing as an Independent, his toying with Hobbism and Cartesianism:

> My thoughtless youth was wing'd with vain desires,
> My manhood, long misled by wandring fires,
> Follow'd false lights; and when their glimps was gone,
> My pride struck out new sparkles of her own.
> Such was I, such by nature still I am,
> Be thine the glory and be mine the shame.

He meant it. Now that Whig historians have had their day it is no longer wildly eccentric to suppose that Dryden's conversion does no damage to his integrity—to believe that he was genuine.

Take, however, the two poets touching on what is, I suppose, the hardest of all theological puzzles, the question of freedom of will as compatible with divine foreknowledge and omnipotence. Milton, the champion of reason, frankly abandons the struggle. In Book 2 of *Paradise Lost* we read of the fallen angels:

> Others apart sat on a Hill retir'd
> In thoughts more elevate, and reason'd high
> Of Providence, Foreknowledge, Will, and Fate,
> Fixt Fate, free will, foreknowledge absolute,
> And found no end, in wandring mazes lost,

a position in which the private judgment will always find itself in discussing that knotty point. In Book 5, Adam raises the difficult question: he asks Raphael:

> But say,
> What meant that caution joind, *if ye be found
> Obedient*? can wee want obedience then
> To him, or possibly his love desert
> Who formd us from the dust, and plac'd us here
> Full to the utmost measure of what bliss
> Human desires can seek or apprehend?

And the Angel, evading the point, replies:

> Son of Heav'n and Earth,
> Attend; That thou art happie, owe to God,
> That thou continu'st such, owe to thy self,
> That is, to thy obedience.

and when he goes on to say that free will is necessary to virtue, without exactly explaining how, all Adam can do is to accept the statement with 'brief gratitude' as Verrall puts it, and at once tactfully go on to ask for the story of the fall of the angels.

But in Act 4 of Dryden's *The State of Innocence*, Adam is full of argument:

> Freedome of will, of all good things is best;
> But can it be by finite man possest?

he asks; and Raphael and Gabriel have a hard time in explaining matters to him. Raphael does not help him much:

> Heav'n by foreknowing what will surely be,
> Does only, first, effects in causes see;
> And finds, but does not make necessity.

and so on: still Adam says,

> I can but choose what he has first design'd
> For he before that choice, my will confin'd:

at which Gabriel gets angry:

> Such impious fancies, where they entrance gain, [he scolds]
> Make Heav'n, all pure, thy crimes to preordain.

whereupon Adam hastily and humbly apologizes:

> Far, far from me be banish'd such a thought:
> I argue only to be better taught.

Nevertheless all the teaching of the archangels leaves him profoundly dissatisfied:

> Hard state of life! Since Heav'n fore-knows my will,
> Why am I not ty'd up from doing ill?
> Why am I trusted with my self at large
> When he's more able to sustain the charge?
> Since angels fell, whose strength was more than mine,
> 'Twould show more grace my frailty to confine.
> Foreknowing the success, to leave me free
> Excuses him, and yet supports not me.

So the argument, we see, has led nowhere: but then Dryden, sceptical of thought, never supposed that it would. Milton's

argument also leads nowhere, but he glozes this over, for we
are to suppose that reason can explain the universe. And if at
the end of the play, Dryden accepts the Resurrection and
Paradise, and does not attempt to explain their necessity in the
scheme of things, that may be attributable to lack of space.

There is one more subject on which both the poets touched
to some extent, Milton in his early days, Dryden with increasing power as he grew older, and that is music, or rather
harmony. Music is that which best represents harmony, and—
the idea is of course the Platonic one—it is through harmony, proportion, that the world was created; it was through
harmony that the world is kept together. It was music, to use
the more specific word, that brought order out of chaos; it was
certain jarring notes that brought about the imperfections of
this world, but at the judgment day all will emerge into a new
and better harmony. Milton, however, only uses this idea as an
illustration: music, for him, was not the essential fact of the
creation—for light was that—but only an agreeable accompaniment. He expresses this idea in the hymn portion of *On the
Morning of Christ's Nativity*:

> Such Musick (as 'tis said)
> Before was never made,
>   But when of old the sons of morning sung,
> While the Creator Great
> His constellations set,
>   And the well-balanc't world on hinges hung,
> And cast the dark foundations deep,
> And bid the weltring waves their oozy channel keep.

Again, in *At a Solemn Musick*, harmony is the accompaniment,
or a result: music is creation's hymn of praise, 'That undis-
turbed Song of pure content,' a song which everything sung,

> As once we did, till disproportion'd sin
> Jarr'd against natures chime, and with harsh din
> Broke the fair musick that all creatures made
> To their great Lord. . . .

With Dryden, however, one gets the impression that it is the vibration of the music itself that brings about the proportion; and it is an idea that he does not treat lightly: he grasped it, made it part of himself with that remarkable capacity he had for making intellectual ideas his own: it has been said that he treats it with awe. The clearest exposition of the idea is in the Grand Chorus of the *Song for St. Cecilia's Day:* it is also the motif of *Alexander's Feast,* but it will suffice to quote the Grand Chorus:

> As from the Pow'r of Sacred Lays
>   The Spheres began to move,
> And sung the great Creator's Praise
>   To all the bless'd above;
> So, when the last and dreadful Hour
> This crumbling Pageant shall devour,
> The TRUMPET shall be heard on high,
> The dead shall live, the living die,
> And MUSICK shall untune the Sky.

It is time, you will think, that I should begin to draw together the somewhat divagating threads of what, I must insist again, are only preliminaries to investigation. This was to have been a comparison and contrast in poetic ideas and poetic method: the ideas, we see, are largely comparable; it is the method that must be contrasted. But as often happens, as perhaps almost inevitably must happen the moment we carry criticism beyond aesthetic rules, beyond, that is to say, dubious abstractions which are in reality no more than signposts; the moment we begin to examine poems from the point of view of the ideas they embody or express, unless we confine ourselves to a consideration of values we are bound to come to questions of personality or character. But we are not, in discussing poetry, interested mainly in such things, at least not as an end: our object is to relate them to the poetry. From the study of poems we come to the poets; from the poets we proceed to discuss poetry itself. Not, I hasten to add, in the hope of clearing up those high insoluble problems which are meat and drink to aesthetic philosophers, but with the prospect of being able to make useful discriminations within poetry, so as not to confuse our judgment of various kinds.

We have in Milton and Dryden two markedly different types of poet: yet they grew from much the same poetic soil, they were affected by much the same influences, they lived in tumultuous times such as cannot fail to leave their mark on those who live through them. Both hankered after writing an epic, though only one did so, unless we consider *Absalom and Achitophel* a minor epic; both were religious poets—for it is time to suggest that Dryden's religious works may outlast his others. Milton was a state official, Dryden took a hand in politics; and moreover they had a number of ideas in common which they used for poetic material. They might have written alike; on any extreme modern theory of literature, they should have written alike: that they did not may serve to illustrate the limitations of such fashionable doctrines.

But they wrote differently; and it was not a question of capacity, because they were both supreme masters of diction. But then one was sublimely egotistic, radically Protestant, touched only by what affected his personal life: the other was detached, Catholic by tendency, apprehending the world through his mind. Milton could only successfully use as material, in either prose or poetry, such things as had seared his emotions, could, in fact, to exaggerate, only be autobiographical. Dryden was not interested in his emotions, and he used best the material he had grasped by means of the intellect: he could, to exaggerate again, be anything but autobiographical. So it was essential for Milton to forge an idiom of his own, which others, naturally, would try to use at their peril: it was equally essential to Dryden to hammer out an idiom for universal use: he reformed our numbers; 'he found the language brick, and left it marble'.

To discuss which of them is the greater poet is invidious:

the answer will depend upon what you expect of poetry, though few, I think, will deny the crown to Milton, who, however, did much damage to the language, while Dryden conferred upon it benefits which are, speaking strictly, inestimable. In that respect, his method is the better. But Milton's purely personal idiom has one great advantage: his poems are, much more than Dryden's, independent objects, complete experiences in themselves: Dryden's, for all their lovely limpidity, as often as not demanded outside reference. Milton paid the price of his glories by being sometimes outrageously distorted and anfractuous: Dryden paid for his masterly statement, for his finality, by needing external support. Milton's method goes deeper, Dryden's is more comprehensive. Whether we think Milton or Dryden has the better method will depend on what we want poetry to do for us: they stand, each of them, at or near the pinnacle of his own particular kind, Milton as a warning, Dryden as a dangerous model.

SIR JOHN VANBRUGH

*Play-writing**

IT was, oddly enough, owing to an incident in his soldier life, that Vanbrugh was able to make fruitful the long months spent in the company of the comic muse in the depths of the Bastille.

It so happened that in his early ensign days, 'when his heart was above his income', he had become 'particularly obliged' to a certain Sir Thomas Skipwith, with whom he was billeted. Cheerful and generous, Sir Thomas, as one of the patentees of the Theatre Royal, Dury Lane, took the responsibilities and chances of the position as carelessly as he did everything else. The finances of the theatre were therefore at a low ebb, and now Vanbrugh was inspired with the idea of repaying his obligation by writing a successful comedy.[1] In any case, even if the play did not take enough to repay his benefactor, it would be an amusing thing to do, and might later bring its reward.

A suitable opportunity arose when in January 1696 the Theatre Royal staged Colley Cibber's first play, *Love's Last Shift*, a comedy which, as Congreve said, had a great many things in it that were like wit, but were not really such. Vanbrugh, on his part, did not find it at all satisfactory from the common-sense point of view. In Cibber's play a virtuous wife

---

* Reprinted from *Essays in Biography 1680–1726*, Oxford University Press, 1925.

[1] Cibber, vi.

reclaims a dissolute husband after a separation of eight years, and the conclusion suggests that they lived happily ever after. To Vanbrugh this seemed absurdly contrary to likelihood, certainly at variance with his own observation of men and women. So as a comment on the moral, as well as to have a good deal of fun of his own, he rapidly wrote a sequel to the play, *The Relapse, or Virtue in Danger*, incidentally raising Sir Novelty Fashion, not only to the peerage, but to a much higher power of comedy. Everybody who read his piece found it highly entertaining, and a more faithful reflection than *Love's Last Shift* not only of the life they knew, but of human nature. However, owing to the lateness of the season—vacation time was near at hand—it was not produced until the end of December, with Cibber in the part of Lord Foppington.

Although the play succeeded by virtue of its raciness and its bold, not to say exaggerated, treatment of actuality, rather than by its literary grace, all the wits at once wanted to know the author. They met a large, fair, handsome man, perhaps a trifle heavy, particularly as to the chin, and with eyes that slanted upwards a little towards the temples. But what charmed them especially was the caressing look in his frank eyes, the smile hovering about his full, shapely lips, and his ready, downright wit. Always cheerful and willing to oblige, good-hearted to a fault, with a robust appreciation of the good things of this life, he took men as he found them, without expecting them to be what they were not, and he liked to be accepted on the same terms.

And accepted he was by the great coterie of elegant writers and notable amateurs—an agreeable and distinguished company, in strong contrast with both his military acquaintance, and the struggling quarrelsome band of actors with whom he had recently come into contact. His fortune was evidently taking a turn for the better. He received the compliments even of that very rising politician, Mr. Montague, London's midwife of letters, who would bring any promising babe into the

literary world, carefully leaving the troublesome and ex-
pensive business of nursing to others. He had read to him some
scenes of the play Vanbrugh had scribbled in the Bastille, and
scenting perhaps another dedication (a form of writing of
which he was inordinately fond) urged him to tack the comedy
together, and give it him for Betterton to act in the other
theatre at Lincoln's Inn Fields. And from this time onward
Captain Vanbrugh was known primarily as a playwright,
everybody, himself included, having apparently forgotten he
was a soldier. Perhaps, however, since campaigning was only
a half-yearly affair, he succeeded in dovetailing professions.

But to be in the public eye, though gratifying, may mean to
be misunderstood, and before Vanbrugh had time even to
print *The Relapse* he was amazed to find himself the object
of attack from certain quarters. Some tiresome people were
beginning to mutter dark things about the theatre, and although Vanbrugh was willing enough to admit that the stage
shared the dual tincture of the rest of life, he could not imagine
why the prudes should set upon him in particular, and accuse
him of 'blasphemy and bawdy'. He was genuinely puzzled.
Blasphemy and Bawdy? for the life of him he could not 'find
'em out' in his play, in which he had with the utmost innocency
of intention portrayed the life of his time. He found himself
compelled to write a preface, so as to point out that a lady of
real reputation might without affront to her prayer-book lay his
volume beside it on her shelf. It was not his fault if people
chose to read sinister meanings into everyday ejaculations.
Surely anybody of sense could see that his sole design in writing
this play had been to please the honest gentlemen of the
town, and 'to divert (if possible) some part of their spleen, in
spite of their wives and taxes'. But there were some who were
not men of sense, 'friends to nobody', saints, 'thorough-paced
ones with screwed faces and wry mouths', men guilty of that
very excess it is the duty as well as the pleasure of every comic
writer to belabour. 'They make debauches in piety', Vanbrugh

declared roundly, 'as sinners do in wine; and are as quarrelsome in their religion, as other people are in their drink; so I hope, nobody will mind what they say.'

But it is difficult to please every variety of person in a complex community, and if the most thorough-paced saint could find nothing against the play Vanbrugh produced at Drury Lane the following January, the less saintly found *Aesop* tedious. It was choke full of morality from beginning to end, and even duller than Boursault's French original. But Chancellor Montague was still urging him to complete his Bastille play, and Vanbrugh felt this was 'a request not to be refused to so eminent a patron of the muses'. So *The Provok'd Wife* was acted in May, and soon afterwards printed. It was as unlike *Aesop* as it is possible to imagine—full of festiveness and frolic, and if not unduly nice as to morality, was no more indecent than the openly lived life of the times. But it had about it an Elizabethan tang, something of that freedom, and even of that wildness, which was disturbing to those who desired a safer, a more sedate world. Vanbrugh, and indeed, most of his contemporaries, thought he was writing plays like Congreve, or any one else; but once again, quite unconsciously, he had thrust his hand into a hornets' nest. For it appeared that his plays were, after all, not like Congreve's, whose chaste example was, at the end of the year, held up for imitation by the doctor-poet Sir Richard Blackmore, who deprecated the 'obscene and profane pollutions' practised upon the stage by other dramatists. Blackmore set the hornets' nest astir, and early in 1698 Merriton published a work on the 'Immorality, Debauchery and Profaneness' of popular amusements. The insects were beginning to sting.

These efforts, however, were mere flea-bitings in comparison with the sulphurous tirade soon afterwards launched into the world under the title of *A Short View of the Profaneness and Immorality of the English Stage, Together with the Sense of Antiquity upon the Argument*. Between its covers ranted Jeremy

Collier, breathing famine and fire, slaughter and desolation, wildly hurling all the brickbats of heaven at the unguarded heads of dramatists, particularly those of Vanbrugh and Congreve, between whom the new Prynne could see no effective difference.

In any case it would not have mattered to him if he had: he had at last found a long-sought opportunity. A non-juring parson dissatisfied with the position accorded his merits in the world, he was consumed by a passion half for notoriety, half for martyrdom. An extremist in religion who revelled in the more dramatic aspects of high Anglican ritual, he had at one time delighted to preach rebellion in crazy pamphlets directed against an Erastian government. He longed to suffer for a cause. When arrested in 1692 on suspicion of complicity in a plot, he had barely been prevailed upon by his friends to accept bail.[1] Even now he was under ban of outlawry for absolving two murderous traitors upon the scaffold. He was, however, no fool, and by no means lacking in erudition; but he was ill-balanced, over-emotional, easily precipitated into violence; and once he saw red he became half demented, rushing into extravagance and dishonesty. And now that the hunt was up he blew his tantivy horn, declared himself huntsman, and halloing on his pack, rode himself desperately back into official grace. For after all, martyrdom when too prolonged is apt to lose its point.

His book fell like a thunderbolt into the coffee-houses and drawing-rooms where art was discussed with intelligence, and life lived reasonably according to the manners of the day. Nobody could quite penetrate the design of this squib, with its absurd confusion of issues; a true jeremiad in style, in which to dally with vice seemed the same sort of crime as to trifle with the Aristotelian unities. Congreve, who had been severely handled, was as much bewildered as hurt; Wycherley was growling angrily in the country; while Dryden, who at his age

[1] Macaulay, *Rest. Dram.*

was not going to allow himself to be much bothered, was contemptuously ready to admit anything, since no admission of the kind Collier sought would affect the literary quality of his plays. The actors, for their part, professed themselves quite at a loss. Everybody knew the stage to be a moral instrument, so why should Collier attack it? They were forced to be content with the solution of the actor Haines, who said that 'Collier himself was a morality mender, and, you know, two of a trade never agree'.[1] Vanbrugh, whose scent seemed to stink hottest in the nose of the pack, could not make head nor tail of all this pother made by one of those very carpers 'with plod shoes, a little band, and greasy hair' against whom he had warned the readers of *The Relapse*. He could not understand why he should be singled out above all others as a monster of depravity. Surely one need not pay much attention; for men of sense would never think any the worse of a play or of its author on account of the mud-slinging of a man 'who runs amuck at all'. No doubt the affair would soon blow over.

The worst of it was, however, that the book achieved instant and enormous popularity. Edition after edition was called for. Collier was hailed as a great reformer, and the decree of outlawry against him allowed to fall into abeyance. Thousands welcomed the book with that acrimonious delight with which the stupid always greet an attack upon their betters in intellect or sensibility. Perhaps also the citizens saw their chance of retaliating upon the heartless playwrights who always made the 'cit' look a goat, and duly supplied him with horns. No doubt Alderman Fondlewife and Alderman Gripe presented copies to their consorts.

Collier certainly knew his public; and moreover the book was vigorously written, and amusing to read, whatever view of art or morality you might hold. And it soon became clear that it was a dangerous book, for early in May the justices of Middlesex 'presented' the playhouses to be 'nurseries of

---

[1] Cibber.

C

debauchery and blasphemy', and they also presented Congreve
for writing *The Double Dealer*, D'Urfey *Don Quixote*, and
Tonson and Briscoe for printing these works. They further
declared that 'women frequenting the playhouses in masks
tended much to debauchery and immorality',[1] a side-issue in
which they were probably right. Indeed, Collier's pack yelped
so noisily that a drowsy and neglected act of James I against
profane swearing,[2] to which the reverend divine had drawn
attention, was put into force. Prosecutions were begun for
lewdness and blasphemy; and informers stationed in the
theatres caught the words from the mouths of the actors, and
carried them red-hot to the justices. It was evident that this
'young histrio-mastix' would have to be answered.

The play from the other side began on the 17th of May
with *A Vindication of the Stage*, perhaps by Wycherley,[3] a light,
amusing piece of writing that had no effect whatever. It was
followed by a volume of Filmer's, not much to the purpose,
being chiefly concerned to show that the Greeks and Romans
were not free from the guilt of having written smutty things.
On the 6th June, however, there appeared the only considerable
answer, by Dennis, the raging critic, who in *The Usefulness of the
Stage* laid stress upon Collier's unfair controversial method,
and also gave the sense of antiquity upon the argument,
turning the tables with some skill. For instance, Collier had
quoted the lines of Ovid which Dryden had translated:

> But above all, the Play-House is the Place;
> There's Choice of Quarry in that narrow Chace.
> There take thy Stand, and sharply looking out,
> Soon mayst thou find a Mistress in the Rout . . .

apropos of which Dennis quoted a little more Ovid anent the
value of Church Parade for the same purpose, and remarked,
'And have we not here a merry person, who brings an

---

[1] Luttrell, 10 and 12 May, 1698.
[2] Ward. For text see Courthope, p. 95.
[3] Gosse, *Congreve*; Macaulay, *Rest. Dram.*

authority against going to theatres, which is as direct against going to church? Nay, and upon the very same account too.' Such hits were telling, but on the whole the book was too learned, and attacked the question from too high an angle of general philosophic aesthetics, to act as an effective counterblast.

The public, indeed, had small time to digest that work, for two days after its issue there appeared *A Short Vindication of The Relapse and the Provok'd Wife*, of course by Vanbrugh, though like the plays it bore no signature. Collier's 'lampoon', he declared, although contemptible enough, was 'now a thing no farther to be laughed at', because it had 'got credit enough to brand the persons it mentions'. But although it must be answered, it was extremely difficult to do so, because Collier's 'play is so wild, I must be content to take the ball as it comes, and return it if I can'. The *Short View* was indeed a slippery thing, for, as Dennis had written with a virulence almost equal to Collier's, the parson was 'so far from having shown in his book either the meekness of a Christian, or the humility of an exemplary pastor, that he has neither the reasoning of a man of sense in it, nor the style of a polite man, nor the sincerity of an honest man, nor the humanity of a gentleman or a man of letters'. Vanbrugh could not hope to equal this Jeremiah Collier in invective, nor would he wish to imitate his florid polemics. He could only oppose the common-sense view of a man of the world, and this, unless handled by a master, offers but meagre resistance to fanatical revilings.

So wild indeed was Collier's play, that not only was it sometimes impossible to see into what part of the court he was aiming the ball, but in some places it was beyond the endeavours of man to take him seriously. To do so, to make too vigorous a defence, might even expose a man to ridicule. What could you make of a fellow who said that the characters in *The Relapse* 'swore in solitude and cold blood, under thought and deliberation, for business and exercise', and declared this to be a

'terrible circumstance', when after all, 'the stretch of the profaneness' lay in Lord Foppington's 'Gad!' and Miss Hoyden's
'Icod!'? 'This', said Vanbrugh, 'is all this gentleman's zeal is in
such a ferment about.' 'Now,' he continued, 'whether such
words are entirely justifiable or not, there's this at least to be
said for 'em: that people of the nicest rank both in their religion and their manners throughout Christendom use 'em.'
That certainly might be a sufficient defence for their use by
frail flesh in daily life, but was it applicable to a work of art?
If Collier attacked a play as though it were a sermon, Vanbrugh defended it as though it might be a speech in Parliament.

But Vanbrugh had done worse than offend against de-
corum, he had jested against the holy order of priests, and the
Reverend Mr. Collier, taking one or two phrases such as
Berinthia's 'Mr. Worthy used you like a text, he took you all
to pieces', brought all his turgid eloquence to bear on the
assault. 'There are few of these last Quotations', he fumed,
'but what are plain Blasphemy, and within the *Law*. They look
reeking from Pandaemonium, and almost smell of Fire and
Brimstone. This is an Eruption of Hell with a Witness! I almost wonder the smoke of it has not darken'd the Sun, and
turned the air to Plague and Poison! These are outrageous
Provocations; enough to arm all Nature in Revenge; to ex-
haust the Judgments of Heaven, and sink the *Island* in the
Sea!' For a simple-minded gentleman, who has merely designed to divert the spleen of his countrymen, to be accused
of nearly bringing the worst horrors of the Apocalypse upon
his native land, must be sore trial—when it gets beyond a
joke—for how can one answer preposterous fustian? Indeed,
at one point Vanbrugh gave up the contest as hopeless, and
resorted to burlesque. When Collier accused him of denying
revealed light by making Amanda say, 'Good Gods, what
slippery stuff are men composed of! Sure the account of the
creation's false, and 'twas the woman's rib they were form'd

of', the vindicator said, 'I'm sorry the gentleman who writ this speech of Amanda's is not here to defend himself; but he being gone away with the Czar, who has made him Poet Laureate of Muscovy . . . &c.', on the principle, no doubt, of answering a fool according to his folly.

Yet Vanbrugh did his best to engage Collier seriously. The divine had laid down that 'The business of plays is to recommend virtue and discountenance vice'. Vanbrugh had thought it was to counteract the depressing effect of wives and taxes, and to get full houses; but since everybody seemed to admit the truth of that part of Collier's argument, he too must rank himself upon the side of the angels. A little thought made it quite plain that *The Relapse* was a tract. Was not its second title *Virtue in Danger*? Slowly he developed the theme that he had been moved to write this play entirely by the touching and satisfactory conclusion of *Love's Last Shift*. He yearned for the happy couple to remain happy; it would be heartbreaking to think of further conjugal misunderstandings. But on the other hand, they must not live in a fool's paradise. Over-confidence might bring temptations. And it was solely to warn them against these temptations, out of a sheer desire for good, that *The Relapse* had been written. Of course the object of plays was to recommend virtue, but how can one discountenance vice without portraying it? 'For the business of comedy is to show people what they should do, by representing them on the stage doing what they should not.' Could any reply be simpler, more triumphant than that?

We need not farther follow this conflict, at once so entertaining and so sad, in which feelings were screwed up to the height of bitterness, and men of intellect failed to answer fools.[1] A host of scribblers sided with Collier against Congreve, and the parson, not content to look on with his sleek smile and supercilious glance, once more rushed into the fray with *A Defence of the Short View*. Like his opponents, he got

[1] See Aitken's *Life of Steele*.

in a few shrewd side blows, but they did nothing to better his case. Indeed, it needed no bettering, for it was already judged. When art and morality are forcibly made bed-fellows, it is usually art that has to yield the place. Certainly on this occasion morality remained in the bed, its pillow smoothed by Addison and Steele, its quilt arranged by Cibber. And as for art, it sought refuge first in the satires of Pope and Swift, and then in the novel. But the result was not brought about all at once. Numbers of pamphlets, signed or anonymous, whitened the booksellers' stalls with their idle leaves, and Dryden wrote a few scathing lines in prologues and epilogues. On the one hand sprung up The Society for the Reformation of Manners, while on the other there appeared in 1699 a timid little sheet modestly showing that swearing and references to child-bearing really had been heard upon the stage before the Restoration.

The controversy rumbled on through the eighteenth century, Dr. Blair declaring that the immorality of *The Provok'd Wife* 'ought to explode it out of decent society', while William Law in 1726,[1] and later the Reverend Doctor John Witherspoon, not so sure of the ballistic qualities of vice, declared the stage an altogether unchristian amusement. But the immediate battle was not confined to words. In November 1701 information was brought against twelve of the players, including Mrs. Barry, Mrs. Bracegirdle, Mr. Betterton, and Mr. Verbruggen, 'for using indecent expressions in some late plays, particularly *The Provok'd Wife*',[2] Betterton and Mrs. Barry being actually fined.[3] Yet these measures were not altogether efficacious in cleansing the heart of the people of London, for as late as about 1706 the author of *Hell upon Earth, or the Language of the Playhouse*, confessed that a public was still attracted by 'horrid comedies'. 'The more they have been exposed by Mr. Collier

---

[1] For an example see Gibbon's *Memoirs of my Life and Writings*, World's Classics, p. 16.
[2] Luttrell V. iii, 20 November, 1701.   [3] Baker.

and others', he lamented, 'the more they seem to be admir'd.'[1] Nevertheless, at the time of Queen Anne's accession the attacks of vexatious busybodies grew so fierce as to endanger the very existence of the theatre, and the Queen herself found it advisable to interfere. She placed the licensing of public shows entirely in the hands of the Master of the Revels, forbade the wearing of masks, and enjoined that 'no Person of what Quality soever, Presume to go Behind the Scenes, or come upon the Stage, either before or during the Acting of Any Play'. For which signal service to the drama, though one which must have interfered not a little with the activities of some of the peers, she received the thanks of the Lords.[2]

---

[1] Quoted by Ward.
[2] Ashton, II. xxv, from Luttrell, 20 January, 1704.

BERNARD MANDEVILLE

*A Letter to Dion**

WHEN a large new class rises to a position where it feels
it is crucial to the life of the nation, it is likely to enquire
into the moral bases of its actions; it is anxious to know, not
only how it should behave, but why it should choose one way
rather than another. And in the extremely lively intellectual
atmosphere of the early eighteenth century, under the stimulus
of the Enlightenment the English became extremely curious
about the motives which actuated them in their daily living.
What induced them to behave well? Why did men indulge in
evil? How far were men guided by their passions? The
general weakening of Christianity brought about by the
writings of such diverse people as Hobbes and Spinoza, the
idea of the mechanical universe which the general mind derived from the Newtonian system, the nature of human understanding as presented by Locke, resulted in a numerous band of
free-thinkers who felt that the ground was cleared for un-
restricted discussion of ethical matters. For them the fear of
divine retribution, the hope of eternal reward, no longer
seemed a sufficient explanation for the impulses towards
good; to some, as to Shaftesbury, such motives were not even
honourable; they degraded the human spirit. Such a discussion naturally took various forms, it existed on several levels
of subtlety, from the crude, if by no means unintelligent anti-

* Introduction to Bernard Mandeville, *A Letter to Dion*, University Press of
Liverpool, 1954.

Christian writings of such men as Toland and Collins, to the more exalted and devout searchings of Berkeley, Butler, and Law, with innumerable smaller fry filling the gaps.

In the eyes of the generally educated man of the period, the 'polite reader', the chief disputants in the field were Mandeville, Shaftesbury, and Berkeley. Those were, moreover, in various degrees, first-rate writers; they could charm and amuse; though they might present extravagances and paradoxes, they appealed ultimately to common sense, that is, to what everybody felt in some way or another within himself. They seemed to be aware of the goings-on in the heart and mind of the average person, and they divided themselves conveniently into two opposing groups—the 'optimists' who believed that man was naturally benevolent, of whom Shaftesbury was the chief, and the 'pessimists' headed by Mandeville, who had come to the conclusion that man was essentially selfish.

Not that the matter was in reality so simple. The optimists had to explain the existence of evil, the pessimists the frequency of noble actions; and looking back on those times from our distance, what strikes us in the extent of the ground common to both parties, which Butler occupied firmly in his *Sermons* (1726). They agreed that a good action was one that was socially good, that men were born with certain impulses, that education modified the natural man; both parties based themselves on the assumption that the only way to make progress in the investigation into morals was to look honestly into one's self; they were in this sense empiricists, and they were not so naïf in psychology as we might flatter ourselves by thinking. And since they were fearlessly introspective, what they had to say is still of enormous importance to us. They raised fundamental issues, and the debate continues on the level of depth-psychology.

For our purpose here the fun began when in 1705 Mandeville published his *The Grumbling Hive*, an entertaining poem in

Hudibrastics arguing that the prosperity of a nation was inevitably connected with luxury and intemperance, that 'Bare
Virtue can't make Nations live in Splendour'. The squib,
embodying an odd version of the then favourite theme of the
Divine Mind 'from seeming evil still educing good', did not
attract much attention; and in the following years Shaftesbury
in stages produced his *Characteristicks* (an unauthorized edition
of his *Inquiry Concerning Virtue and Merit* had appeared as early
as 1699). It is of course too easy a simplification to say that he
believed that men were naturally benevolent, social, and virtuous by instinct, but that is what his philosophy amounted to
in the popular view. To Mandeville, the latest in the long line
of genial cynics, tracing his descent from Montaigne, Bayle,
and La Rochefoucauld, such a view was contrary to all experience. As a doctor, a specialist in nervous diseases, he
knew better. '[Shaftesbury's] notions, I confess,' he remarked
blandly, 'are generous and refined: they are a high compliment to human kind . . . What a pity it is they are not true.'

The irritation caused by these, to him, absurdities, led him
in 1714 to compile a considerable treatise, *The Fable of the
Bees: or, Private Vices, Publick Benefits*, in which the various
statements of his original poem are explained at length in racy
vernacular prose, the expansion of his thought being preceded by 'An Enquiry into the Origin of Moral Virtue'. This,
of course, was what the whole controversy was about, not
economics. Although there was a second edition in that year,
it raised little notable comment until its reissue in 1723, when
there were added 'An Essay on Charity and Charity Schools',
and 'A Search into the Nature of Society'. These, being para-
doxical in statement, and too true to be altogether pleasant, the
work as a whole now roused a frenzied furore of indignation; not only was the book twice 'presented' to the jury of
Middlesex as a public nuisance, it was also inveighed against
in pulpit and press, the papers being reinforced by a whole
flutter of pamphlets, the majority of protests coming from

those who had probably not read the book, and certainly did not understand it. It was, to be sure, easy to misrepresent; and as it attacked the vanity of most normally self-approving men —no man, for instance, who is charitable, likes to be told that 'thousands give money to beggars from the same motive as they pay their corn-cutters, to walk easy'—it caused unpleasant heart-searchings. The work thus bidding fair to become a dangerous undermining of all self-esteem, the replies were in the main stupidly violent, though some, notably those by Hutcheson and William Law, were by no means negligible. Mandeville answered one attack, but otherwise took no individual notice of them: but in 1729 he issued a bulky 'Second Part' in dialogue form—one of his interlocutors having been misled by the critics—in which he stated his position a little more soberly. Then in 1732 Berkeley published the brilliant collection of dialogues which he had composed on Rhode Island, *Alciphron: or the Minute Philosopher*, in the second of which his free-thinkers, Alciphron and Lysicles, supposedly upholding the principles of *The Fable of the Bees*, are made to look 'prating, light, vain, superstitious', in all, a good deal more than ridiculous.

Much as one may admire Berkeley, it must be confessed that here he didn't play altogether fair. He was (one suspects) enjoying himself too much. He seemed indeed to have realized that he was giving undue rein to an amused imagination, since in the 'Advertisement' which precedes his second edition, he remarked:

> ... It must not ... be thought that authors are misrepresented, if every notion of Alciphron or Lysicles is not found precisely in them. A gentleman in private conference, may be supposed to speak plainer than others write, to improve on their hints, and draw conclusions from their principles.

But you cannot, as 'conclusions', draw from *The Fable of the Bees* the 'principles' that Lysicles offered as being so beneficial to happiness. Mandeville emphatically did not say that vice was preferable to virtue. On the contrary, he had declared:

> When I assert that vices are inseparable from great and potent societies, and that it is impossible that wealth and grandeur should subsist without, I do not say that the particular members of them who are guilty of any should not be continually reproved, or not punished for them when they grow into crimes.

It had, however, to be understood that when he pronounced all men to be vicious, he was taking up the extreme 'rigoristic' point of view, namely that anything you did to please yourself came under the head of 'vice', the essence of 'virtue' being self-denial. Thus when he maintained that private vices were public benefits, he was only saying that if men didn't spend their money on pleasure, there would be little wealth in the nation, no trade, no arts, and a chronic condition of unemployment. And, after all, Berkeley himself admitted as much when he asked later in *The Querist*, that astonishingly advanced treatise on economics:

> Whether the ornaments and furniture of a good house do not employ a number of all sorts of artificers, in iron, wood, marble, brass, pewter, copper, wool, flax, and divers other materials?
> Whether in buildings and gardens a great number of day-labourers do not find employment?

And again, when Berkeley made Lysicles childishly absurd by seeming to uphold licentious dissipation as the ultimate good, and self-interest as the only respectable motive of action, he might have remembered that some thirty years earlier he had jotted down in his *Commonplace Book* (not published till last century), that 'Sensual pleasure is the *summum bonum*. This the great principle of morality': and 'I'd never blame a man for acting upon interest. He's a fool that acts on any other principles.'

For, of course, Mandeville no more than Berkeley thought with Lysicles that the major delights of life were those of whoring, drunkenness, and dicing; both believed that the most satisfying pleasure was a good conscience based on the performance of worthy actions; where they differed was in the motive. For Mandeville 'the moral virtues are the political offspring which flattery begot upon pride', which Berkeley as a good Churchman, apart from anything else, could not accept. But put the remarks of either in the context of their whole thought, and each comes out as a sound, common-sense moralist. So what goaded the ageing Mandeville into a reply was the assumption that anyone who agreed with him in any way was a vapid-minded, idle profligate; whereas, whatever might be said about Mandeville, it was clear that he was, in Dr. Johnson's phrase, 'a thinking man', and a conscientious citizen. So addressing himself to Dion as writer of the letters describing the conversations of the minute philosophers, he produced a dignified rebuke, together with a restatement of his position. The *Letter to Dion* is really part of the corpus of the *Fable;* but since the refutation of the *Alciphron* dialogue almost necessarily involves extensive quotation from the *Fable*, Mr. F. B. Kaye, when he edited it, together with the most brilliant and penetrating commentary that has yet appeared, omitted the *Letter* from his two already large volumes.

But seeing that *A Letter to Dion* contains a good deal of fresh and characteristic writing, and has never been reprinted, it has been thought worth while to make it easily available to the reader today. It is true that Mandeville seems here and there to flag a little—after all, he was over sixty—but how trenchant his strokes still often are, how the wit still pierces the weighty argument! And all the while there is revealed the ultimate trust in human nature that was really at the base of this apparently cynical critic of mankind, who wrote, as he said, 'without rancour or peevishness'. Clear your mind of cant, he seems to say, throw overboard even the most apparently glorious reasons for self-approbation, and you will find that you are not really so bad after all, and society is still perfectly liveable.

DANIEL DEFOE*

You will have wondered, perhaps, why I have chosen to speak to you in Spring 1946 about Daniel Defoe. I have thought him an appropriate figure to discuss, because the situation in which he found himself enmeshed as an Englishman bears many resemblances, though indeed in a milder form, to that in which many Europeans now see themselves caught. I have felt him to be in some measure symbolic, a progressive man, filled with an ardour to do good, baffled, persecuted, poverty-haunted, yet by genius and persistence triumphing in a way he never dreamt of. For the England of his day was an England of emergence; the England he was born into was a country in the throes of a revolution; a profound social reorganization was taking place. He lived through an age of political adjustment, of embittered faction expressing itself in private violence and popular turbulence; so what takes shape before us as we study Defoe is the picture of a very unusual man battling furiously through dangerous storms, coming out at last into a kind of uneasy anchorage, having, as though by accident, created new literary forms. In spite of his intensely practical life of business, harried by misfortune to the very last, he invented the modern novel, the great literary vehicle of the middle classes for over two hundred years. I will not dwell upon that now. Virginia Woolf, at least, a reliable witness in this field, talks of him as 'the predecessor of Richardson and Fielding, one of the first indeed to shape the novel and launch it on its way'.

* A lecture delivered at Amsterdam to the Allard-Pierson Stichting, Afdeling voor Moderne Literatuurwetenschap, *Neophilologus*, Vol. xxx, 1946.

He was indeed astonishingly seminal. Without his pioneering efforts, unpolished as they were, Steele and Addison would never have achieved their fame in essay-writing; again, towards the end of his life, he was to invent the leading article in the newspaper. But to get a glimpse of the abundance of his ideas we must turn for a moment to see the kind of man he was, a man who contrived to be, as Mr. W. P. Trent has said, 'an important politician as well as an influential journalist . . . one of the best-known of all Englishmen during the reigns of William III, Anne, and George I. He was, moreover, a historian, a biographer, a poet, an essayist, a political economist, a sociologist, a religious controversialist, a moralist, a writer on occult subjects', and we might add (*excusez du peu!*) a military strategist on an imaginative scale, and a stout advocate of women's rights. 'In short', as Mr. Trent concludes, 'a Proteus both in literature and affairs, who, when he is viewed in the light of the totality of his powers and performances, seems to be an almost titanic genius.'

Anyone curious about the nature, or the quality, of Defoe's writings is inevitably led to pay some attention to his life, because almost the whole of Defoe's existence seems to fit into a straggling pattern of apprenticeship, which fitted him at the age of about sixty to scribble off at top speed, one after the other, those copious, varied masterpieces which gain rather than lose in significance as time goes on. His social milieu, his successes, his misfortunes, the tasks to which chance set him, all appear in retrospect providentially designed to bring about the destined result—given, of course, his personal gifts. Yet these last were not such as we would call markedly literary. It is true that as a young man he was ambitious to be a poet; but few of those who share this not uncommon desire can have produced such execrably bad verse as Defoe was guilty of in a political poem of 1691: he was, to be sure, a member of that society which gathered round those first hesitating steps in popular culture, Dunton's *Athenian Gazette* and *Athenian*

Mercury; but for sheer grotesqueness his pindarics eclipse even the gawkiest of those to be discovered there. Indeed he was no poet, though he had a considerable talent for lively, telling topical verse, which slipped off his pen with fabulous ease. 'By his writing a poem every day', Dunton was to remark later, 'one would think that he rhymed in his sleep.' No one now, except the ardent student of Defoe, will read more than his two most famous pieces of verse, *The True-Born Englishman* and the *Hymn to the Pillory;* they will skim over the verses in the third part of *Robinson Crusoe* (Defoe, we see, went on writing verse to the end), and will avert their eyes from the twelve portentous books, no less, of *Jura Divino,* which Defoe wrote in 1706, and which deals, sometimes scathingly enough, with opponents of the Hanoverian Succession.

He certainly had no ambition to be a distinguished writer of prose. 'As to language', he tells us at the end of his first considerable work, the *Essay on Projects* of 1698, a somewhat visionary, though avowedly downright utilitarian work, 'As to language, I have been rather careful to make it speak English suitable to the manner of the story, than to dress it up with the exactness of style: choosing rather to have it free and familiar . . . than to strain at a perfection of language which I rather wish for than pretend to be master of.' He was, we can now see, an active agent in that movement which broke away from prose written for the aristocracy, to that written for the man in the street, for the new reading public which was so remarkable a symptom of the profound social change transforming England. This prose was to become in his hands the perfect instrument for the kind of thing which, twenty years later, he was going to do so brilliantly.

It was not Defoe's conscious desires that made him what he became; he wished for nothing better than to be a poet and a successful merchant: he was neither. But the little twist of brain that constitutes him a genius was given its field by the fact that he was indeed a manufacturing tradesman, and that

D

Fate had caused him to be born of dissenting parents. The shape of his life, and the nature of most of his works, if not of all, flow from those facts. He was indeed possessed of, one might even say daemonically possessed by, an inexhaustible energy; and, as was almost bound to happen in those days, his energy drove him into politics; but it was because he was a tradesman that he played the part that he did; it was because he was a dissenter that so much of his work is coloured in the way that it is. I may perhaps linger a moment over his really extraordinary vital force, since vitality in one form or another is an essential part of creative greatness. One would think that the two hundred and fifty odd works which appeared with his name, some of them considerably bulky; the literally unnumbered pamphlets and articles which poured out from him; his newspaper, the *Review*, written entirely by his own hand for some ten years, would have meant passing a lifetime chained to a writing table. Not a bit of it! When one thinks of Defoe, one must visualize a small man with brown hair covered by a wig, a sharp chin and a mole near his mouth, incessantly flitting up and down across Great Britain, engaged on political work or journalistic forays. When you expect to find him in London editing his *Review*, he will be in Scotland helping to bring about the union of the two kingdoms. If you look for him in Norfolk, where under the guise of judging crops he should be engaged in politics, you will hear that he is at Bristol interviewing the famous castaway Alexander Selkirk. We get the impression of a furious piece of nuclear energy, never still, yet always writing, writing, writing.

It is possible that had he been a successful hosier instead of going bankrupt in 1692, he would have written much less, and none of the works we now revere him for: nevertheless his early writing brought into play two qualities which he possessed in overplus, journalistic rather than literary qualities, which would no doubt have struggled for outlet. The first is a passion for, and uncanny skill in, observing fact; no detail escaped his eye. The second is a memory which seems never to have let anything slip. It is more than likely that the grimly realistic scenes of the *Journal of the Plague Year* written in 1722, are the fruits of the memory of an old man harvesting the minute observations of a dauntlessly inquisitive little cockney five or six years old roaming the horror-infested streets of London in 1665. It is these qualities of observation and memory which, developed to the height that they were, determined the class of literary genius to which Defoe was to belong.

For his creative imagination—it is here that his first literary quality appears—always worked best in the realm of fact. His utilitarian *Essay on Projects*, which I have already mentioned, deals entirely with practical affairs; but they are handled with an imagination so staggering that we have only lately caught up with it: in the matter of roads, for instance, of old age pensions, of women's colleges. It is because Defoe was a practical man of affairs, so long immersed in business, that *Robinson Crusoe* is what it is. Crusoe is all the time a tradesman, forever collecting goods, taking stock, planning ahead: his island becomes one enormous business enterprise, a vast emporium of goods, just as Defoe's brain was a repository brimful of memories.

One striking example where we can directly trace the literary result to the practical source occurs readily to the mind. From 1695 to 1699, Defoe was a commissioner of the glass duty; routine no doubt compelled visits to glass factories, but when there Defoe gave full rein to his intense journalistic curiosity. His memory of these visits enabled him a quarter of a century later, in 1722, to write those inimitable pages in his *Colonel Jack* where he describes how the ragamuffins of London, the 'dirty little glass-bottle-house boys', made these factories their homes: 'we all made shift', Jack tells us, 'though we were so little, to keep from starving; and as for lodging . . . in winter we got into the ash-holes, and nealing-arches in the

glass-house. . . .' And then a more particular memory—or was
it imagination?—dictates a telling piece of detail: 'I remember
that one cold winter night we were disturbed in our rest with a
constable and his watch, crying out for one Wry-neck, who it
seems had done some roguery, and required a hue and cry of
that kind; and the watch were informed that he was to be
found among the beggar-boys under the nealing-arches in the
glass-house.

'The alarm being given, we were awakened in the dead of
night, with, Come out here, ye crew of young devils, come out
and show yourselves; so we were all produced: some came out
rubbing their eyes, and scratching their heads, and others were
dragged out.' It seems that there were about seventeen in all,
dislodged from their 'warm apartment among the coal-ashes'.

But if being a man of affairs was one of the moulding
agencies in the life of Defoe as a writer, his being a dissenter,
not of the national state-endowed Church, was of equal, if not
of greater importance. It affected his attitude, political as well
as religious, determined the whole course of his life, and gave
his writings their very definite tone. His religious outlook was
that of his class, the well-to-do middle class large tradesman,
which exalted the virtues of hard work and thrift—which had
their reward in this world as well as the next—regarded all
pleasure with suspicion, laid stress on the puritan values, and
richly enjoyed repentance. They liked to live in a continual
glow of self-righteousness; Robinson Crusoe, we notice, is
often intolerably self-righteous. But what is of most significance for us in Defoe's religion is that it generated in him a
sense of isolation, of being alone in a hostile world, a sense
from the first exaggerated in him, and which his subsequent
adventures were to intensify beyond reason. Dissenters, it is
true, were barred from many privileges and activities; they
were denied entry to universities, they could not enter Parliament, nor become important state functionaries; unless indeed they allowed themselves the subterfuge of 'occasional

conformity', that is, of varying their regular attendance at chapel with the legal requirements of church-going. But with this happy solution, this getting the best of both worlds, Defoe would have no truck. He would not bow down in the house of Rimmon, and by continually attacking the practice embroiled himself disastrously with his own community.

Politically, being a dissenter made him a Whig, an ardent supporter of the revolution and of William of Orange, to whom he was devoted. In one of his poetic flights, where he describes the king's death and his voyage into heaven, he says ecstatically:

> A guard of glorious lights form'd his ascent,
> And wond'ring stars adored him as he went.
> (Jure Divino)

At one time, indeed, he had been a confidant of the King, under whom he bade fair to flourish. And Defoe's great popular triumph as a writer arose out of his advocacy of William III. When the opposition, piqued by the King's success, hating his foreign policy, jealous of the Dutchmen he was naturally inclined to rely on as advisers, raised a cry of England for the English, and vaunted the merits of the true-born Englishman, Defoe rushed to the rescue. Himself possibly of Flemish extraction, he was something of an internationalist—his lack of national prejudice is visible in many of his novels—he turned on those who made ridiculous pretensions for the English, and, in brisk, spirited verse had no difficulty in showing that:

> A true-born Englishman's a contradiction,
> In speech an irony, in fact a fiction;

which is just as well if you accept his picture of the ruling aristocracy who raised the cry:

> These are the heroes who despise the Dutch,
> And rail at new-come foreigners so much;

> Forgetting that themselves are all derived
> From the most scoundrel race that ever lived;
> A horrid crowd of rambling thieves and drones,
> Who ransacked kingdoms, and dispeopled towns.

The whole poem, which is something more than doggerel, moves so trippingly, is so full of common sense, sparkles with so many neat thrusts at those vain of their origin, that it provoked huge gusts of laughter. Besides, from the very beginning it offered so much satirical amusement, carried you along so easily, that everybody who could read at all devoured it; those who could not read had it read to them, as the common custom then was. Who could resist the rollicking lilt of:

> Dutch Walloons, Flemings, Irishmen and Scots,
> Vaudois and Valtolins and Huguenots,
> In good Queen Bess's charitable reign,
> Supplied us with three hundred thousand men:
> Religion—God we thank thee!—sent them hither,
> Priests, Protestants, the devil, and all together.

It swung opinion completely round: nobody afterwards dared to boast himself a true-born Englishman for fear of the shower of ridicule that would be sure to descend upon him at the statement.

Defoe was rapidly recovering from his bankruptcy when William died, and the country was plunged into a period of pitiless faction, at times dangerously approaching civil war, into a struggle where, as usual, politics and religion were inextricably intermingled. The landed interest, Toryism, and the Divine Right of Kings, clashed with commerce and Whiggery supported by Dissent. Defoe, eager politician that he was, partisan dissenter from the first, could not keep out of the turmoil, and so courted his downfall. On the accession of Anne, the Tory High-Church party plucked up courage, and, egged on by the preacher Sacheverell, who raised what he called 'the bloody flag and banner of defiance', engaged in a double campaign against the dissenters, on the one hand of vituperation, on the other of political action in the form of Bills to put an end to occasional conformity. Defoe, who in the previous decade had shot out more than one pamphlet on these matters, once more entered the lists with a brilliant squib called *The Shortest Way with the Dissenters*.

It was in this work that he first revealed that element in his genius which, we may well think, is his most distinctive mark: that capacity so to enter into the being of a person he is portraying as seemingly to become that person, to have that person's emotions, to speak with his or her authentic voice. It is one of the faculties Wordsworth gives the poet, who will wish, he says, 'to bring his feelings near to those of the person he describes, nay, for short spaces of time, perhaps, let himself slip into an entire delusion, and even confound and identify his own feelings with theirs'. It is this faculty which makes Robinson Crusoe, the saddler of the *Journal of the Plague Year*, Moll Flanders and a dozen others, people in whose reality you believe, and which makes enduring the books which contain them. It is the creative imagination working on actuality raised to the highest pitch; it seems almost to be the complete transference of Defoe's self into his creatures.

In his pamphlet he projected himself into the soul of a 'high-flyer', as extreme members of the Church party were called; and he spoke so perfectly as a high-flyer would, that the work was hailed with vociferous delight by the more fanatical members of that sect, who believed *The Shortest Way* to be written by one of themselves. Defoe, indeed, artist that he was, made some of the argument so plausible, and the whole structure so logical, that we need not be surprised that most readers, as Defoe later complained, missed the scalding irony. 'We hang men for trifles', he said, quite justly, since in those days petty theft was a hanging matter, 'and banish them for things not worth naming; but an offence against God and the Church, against the welfare of the world and the dignity of religion, shall be bought off for five shillings.' To us it all appears a monstrous fantasy, the irony we would think obvious. Could anyone, we ask, apply to dissenters, literally, such passages as ' . . . it is cruelty to kill a snake or toad in cold blood, but the poison of their natures makes it a charity to our neighbours to destroy such creatures, not for any personal injury received, but for prevention; not for the evil they have done, but the evil they may do': or, 'If one severe law were made and punctually executed, that whoever was found at a conventicle should be banished the nation, and the preacher hanged, we should soon see an end of the tale'. Yet this outrageous document was taken seriously by both sides: one young parson wrote to a friend that he valued it next to the Bible and the Commandments, and he hoped that the Queen would act on the suggestions contained in it. The dissenters, conversely, were panic-stricken.

The pamphlet, then, created a furore, only made worse for Defoe by his *Brief Explanation*, for both sides now looked upon him as their enemy. His political foes took the opportunity of having the book declared a seditious libel, and a reward was offered for the writer's apprehension. Defoe went into hiding, but soon gave himself up to save the printer, and was flung into the notorious prison at Newgate. The blow was in every way crushing. It meant the ruin of the flourishing pantile business which was to have been his salvation; it meant the relegation of his family to poverty; it might mean transportation; it certainly meant—and this was the most desolating thing—that he would for ever be despised, be subject to contumely. He was condemned to remain in prison at the Queen's pleasure; worst of all, to his agonised dismay, he was sentenced to stand three times in the pillory. He dreaded this horrible indignity more than anything, even more than transportation: but seeing that it was inescapable, with magnificent courage he wrote his *Hymn to the Pillory*, a

defiant taunt to his enemies. 'Tell them', he commands the
pillory at the end of the poem:

> Tell them the Men that placed him there,
> Are Scandals to the Times;
> Are at a loss to find his Guilt,
> And can't commit his Crimes.

Fortune rewards the brave; and, astonishingly, his appearance in the pillory, far from being a humiliation, was a public
triumph. The mob, instead of pelting him with filth, decked
the scaffolding with garlands of flowers, boisterously drank
his health, and when he came down, gave him food and drink.

But public acclamation did not save his business, nor wash
him clean of the sense of degradation; for years he was never
free of debt; he lived in terror of imprisonment. Most to our
purpose here, however, as enquirers into his work, is that it
increased his sense of isolation; he never again felt, as far as we
can judge, that he was a full, and fully free, member of the
society he so fervently wished to benefit. It is, indeed, curious,
and I think noteworthy, that he appears to have had no
personal friends. He belonged to none of the literary coteries
of his day. Not only none of the great, but none of the lesser
fry seem to have known him—except as an object of vilifica-
tion; Swift even putting upon him the crowning insult of
pretending to have forgotten his name! One cannot avoid
concluding that he came to be possessed by what we would
call 'persecution mania', and was filled with an abiding sense
that he was never given a chance. In a passage in the third part
of *Robinson Crusoe*, 'The Serious Reflections', he tells '*too
feelingly*', he italicises the words, of men who have experienced
'the universal contempt of mankind . . . borne down by
calumny and reproach'. This part of the work, much of it so
evidently autobiographical, is direct evidence that Defoe never
threw off the sense of being a pariah. Is it not significant—and
here is the interest in his life for us as literary critics—that the

major characters in his later, his great work, those characters who tell us their story, are all of them in one way or another outcasts; and except for Robinson Crusoe, in a way the type and symbol of them all, open to 'the universal contempt of mankind'?

The second capital consequence of his imprisonment was his being plunged for the remainder of his life into journalism and paid political work, which his enemies called spying. Thanks to the solicitations of high politicians, only too ready to hire so obviously effective a pen, solicitations backed by promises of release and protection, not to say funds, he embarked upon his amazing journalistic production, the *Review*. Its interest is not for the historian alone, nor for the historian of literature merely as it illustrates the development of the essay, but also for the student of Defoe as a writer. For in it we see his style gradually attaining that flexible colloquial quality which is a mark of his later writing. We see it change under our eyes. It was a hard apprenticeship, a rigorous discipline, without which the later masterpieces would not live as they so largely do by their engaging ease of utterance. His political work too was of literary service. It sent him over every part of the country, to mix with all sorts of people, in large houses, on the roads, in inns, in factories, in cottages; it gave him that detailed knowledge of the way people live, or 'make do', thus animating his works with characters of great variety, besides giving him the material to compile one of the best and liveliest of travel-books, *A Journey through England and Wales*.

Perhaps the first sign of his gifts as a really creative writer is that enchanting little masterpiece—one cannot deny it the name—*A True Relation of the Apparition of Mrs. Veal, the next Day after her Death, to one Mrs. Bargrave at Canterbury, the 8th of September, 1705*. It first appeared as an appendix to an edition of the much read book on death by Drelincourt, and was long considered a comment on it, even a sceptical one.

But Defoe had a firm faith in apparitions, and we know now that a story of that sort was actually current, and that Defoe, impelled by his journalistic flair, had dashed down to Canterbury to get what today we call 'a hot story'. Yet whether we regard the little work as a piece of accurate and inspired journalism, or look upon it as a piece of equally inspired invention—with Defoe it is always impossible to disentangle fact from fiction—the result is an indubitable gem. We know from the title what sort of story we are to be told, and, with extraordinary art, Defoe from the very beginning gives us solid ground to stand on; the verisimility he thrusts upon us compels us to accept his veracity. To give us confidence, he tells us first that Mrs. Bargrave, to whom the ghost appeared, is his intimate friend; he can 'avouch for her reputation for the last fifteen or sixteen years'—note the cunning of the indefinite date. Then he assures us that she is not at all of what we should call the 'psychic' type; she is a perfectly normal, cheerful person. 'Notwithstanding', he tells us, 'the ill-usage of a very wicked husband, there is not the least sign of dejection in her face.'

And then, when the evidence, as vouched for by Mrs. Bargrave, is passed on to us, the very things which go to show that the appearance of Mrs. Veal was supernatural are almost glozed over. The details are given so delicately, with such supreme tact, that unless we are alert we will hardly notice them; they are given as part of the ordinary, matter-of-fact story which only a fool would think of doubting: the supernatural is treated on a level with the commonplace, thus giving it all the reality of an everyday occurrence. It is really only at the end, on thinking the matter over, that the occult points occur to us: namely that Mrs. Bargrave never actually touched her friend, so did not doubt her fleshly solidity. She did indeed ask to kiss her, 'which Mrs. Veal complied with, till their lips almost touched; and then Mrs. Veal drew her hand across her own eyes and said, "I am not very well", and so waived it'.

Evidently she remembered just in time that she was a ghost; or else she was a very crafty one! Again, Mrs. Veal would not hold the book she had asked her friend to fetch; instead, she asked Mrs. Bargrave to read it aloud to her. Ghosts, we conclude, cannot hold books. I do not know whether the event was miraculous: I am only sure that the work of art, beyond contradiction, is.

I have dwelt upon this little piece because there already we see Defoe's method fully developed. First we get every circumstance adduced to ensure that we shall feel the book to be true; invention, lying, we must understand, is contrary to every Puritan principle. Then we have the significant facts presented almost as asides, irrelevancies, as things nobody would bother to invent, or tell a lie about. Those are the two pillars of Defoe's craft. And I have dwelt upon it also because it illustrates another thread constantly running through much of Defoe's work, his preoccupation with the occult, that odd streak of mysticism, which crops up strangely in places where it is least expected, not only in the 'Vision of the Angelick World', which concludes *Robinson Crusoe*, but, for example, in the book itself, and, of all places, in the make-up of that materialistic old sinner, Moll Flanders, of whom I shall speak in a few moments.

I must now leap over intervening years to the period beginning in 1719, during which Defoe wrote his novels, beginning with *Robinson Crusoe*. At the outset we are faced with an awkward question: if, as perhaps you will grant for the moment, the material of the novel is man living within society, how can we say that *Robinson Crusoe* is a novel? Here is the story of a man separated from society, a story which achieved its instant popularity from being a tale of adventure built up of those matter-of-fact details so dear to an age which, for about twenty-five years, cared for no writing that was not practical. I am speaking of the mass of readers. But still it is, one would think, essentially a tale of solitude—as, I may remind you, all Defoe's stories are, though except for this one they are all of solitude within society. We can find our justification in Rousseau, the first to see in it a philosophic as opposed to an adventure story, or even as opposed to the moral story Defoe always contended that it was. *Robinson Crusoe*, you may remember, was the only book Émile was to be allowed to read; it was for a long time to constitute his whole library. 'I admit', Rousseau says, 'that the condition of being on a desert island is not that of social man: it is [he adds charmingly] most unlikely to be Émile's lot; but it is through this very condition that he must appreciate all other conditions. The surest way to raise one's self above prejudice, and to work out one's judgment as to the true relation between things, is to put one's self into the position of an isolated man, and to judge all things as such a man must judge them. . . .' (*Émile*. Livre III.)

It is, of course, the fascinating book of our childhood: what we have to ask ourselves as we grow older is, does it still fascinate us? Does Rousseau's philosophic implication prevent us being submerged under the too great wealth of material detail? I would say, yes, and no. Rousseau helps us a little, I have no doubt; but what will help us most is an attentive reading, so as not to miss the little suggestions, the large implications, which Defoe constantly offers us. Only so can we catch the seemingly artless irony which he infuses into his story, so slyly, one imagines, because he wishes to cheat the eye of the puritanical inquisitor. One always has to read Defoe attentively, if one is to reap the whole harvest of his peculiar mind. Here, ostensibly, we have the daily doings and thoughts of a respectable God-fearing business man, earning prosperity because of his industry, and his observance of the Sabbath. Ordinary enough, you will say; but see how deftly the major, unacknowledged preoccupation is suggested. Take the passage where Crusoe has been salvaging things from the wreck: in one drawer he found several useful articles, such as razors,

knives and forks; and in another he found 'about thirty-six
pounds value in money, some European coin, some Brazil,
some pieces of eight, some gold, some silver'—we are spared
no detail. And then: 'I smiled to myself at the sight of this
money. "O drug!" said I aloud, "what art thou good for?
Thou art not worth to me, no, not the taking off of the ground;
one of these knives is worth all this heap. I have no manner of
use for thee; even remain where thou art, and go to the bottom
as a creature whose life is not worth saving." However, upon
second thoughts, I took it away; and wrapping all this in a
piece of canvas, I began to think of making another raft. . . .'
What a splendid stroke, of psychology and of social criticism!
No spoken comment, just a semicolon between 'took it away'
and 'and wrapping it all up . . .' The passage called forth
Coleridge's admiration. 'Worthy of Shakespeare!' he exclaims:
'—and yet the simple semicolon after it,[1] the instant passing
on without the least pause of reflex consciousness, is more
exquisite and masterlike than the touch itself. A meaner writer,
a Marmontel, would have put an (!) after "away", and have
commenced a fresh paragraph'. And indeed one of the constant pleasures in reading Defoe is to catch the irony, so easily
missed, or a criticism sometimes almost Swiftian in its
devastating completeness, both so shyly hidden away, that
if such things did not occur so often one might imagine them
to be accidental.

But yet, you will say, even after running across a dozen
such instances—where Crusoe prays for the first time and at
once gets drunk on the tobacco-impregnated rum; where,
finding himself able to strut about under an umbrella he thanks
Providence for its goodness—yet, you will ask, is this a novel?
Does it, with its underlying insistence upon trade, its material-
ism shot with moral reflections, its endless detail punctuated
with irony, work on us in the same way that a novel does?
Like all Defoe's fiction it is quite formless; it just starts and

---

[1] Unluckily in the first edition it is a comma! (Ed.)

goes on to the end; there is no change of speed, no preparation for a scene followed by the scene, no climax, and therefore no emotional node. You may declare, if you like, with Rousseau, that it is a study of society: but does that society bear any relation to our notion of what man in society is like? Does it place man in any sort of perspective? Let us listen to Virginia Woolf, who is discussing this very aspect of the problem. The idea of a desert island, she says, leads you to expect romantic scenery, the sun rising and setting, man brooding in solitude upon man. 'We read', she goes on, 'and we are rudely contradicted on every page. There are no sunsets and no sunrises; there is no solitude and no soul. There is, on the contrary, staring us full in the face, nothing but a large earthenware pot.' It is the method he had used for Mrs. Veal, and it seems unpromising enough for a novel; but this is how, after discussion, Mrs. Woolf concludes: 'Thus Defoe, by reiterating that nothing but a plain earthenware pot stands in the foreground, persuades us to see remote islands and the solitudes of the human soul. By believing fixedly in the solidity of the pot and its earthiness, he has subdued every element to his design; he has roped the whole universe into harmony. And is there any reason, we ask as we shut the book, why the perspective that a plain earthenware pot exacts should not satisfy us as completely, once we grasp it, as man himself in all his sublimity standing against a background of broken mountains and tumbling oceans with stars flaming in the sky?'

It all depends from where you look at it; for us, living at the last ebb of the romantic movement, it is not easy to grasp it. Perhaps before we can glimpse the perspective of this book, we have to allow ourselves to be caught up in the world of *Moll Flanders*, a greater work, some will think, than *Robinson Crusoe*. It is not to be read by children; indeed in Victorian days it was regarded as quite unsuitable to lie on the drawing-room table. Moll Flanders herself is a creature entirely realized; and not only is this wicked, jolly, imperfectly repentant old woman completely alive, but she is, somehow, completely good. She behaved as she did, we are led to believe, became what she was, because, society being what it is, she could have behaved in no other way. Her enjoyment, her sense of glory, her ineffectual fits of remorse, her shrewd comment, her immense talent for lying offset by her rare genius for telling the truth (in these last she is like Defoe himself), her human affections with their intermittences, the way she tells it all, endear the sinful old creature to us. No doubt Defoe, with one part of his mind, designed her as a warning; he says, of course, in his preface, as was his custom, that this is a moral tale: he regarded all his fiction, he never wearies of telling us, as a blow in the battle for the reformation of manners. Perhaps he really meant this. But as he worked, scribbling away at unbelievable speed, growing into the skin of his character, something else took charge—the creative faculty: some glow other than that of moral virtue suffused him, the glow of the artist rejoicing in his work. Whatever the cause, *The Fortunes and Misfortunes of Moll Flanders* is a book of first-rate importance.

For it marks the birth of the modern novel. It is a large claim, I know, but it can be argued, if, as I would suggest, the peculiar mark of the novel as an art form distinct from other literary forms, is that it shows the individual in society, reveals society to itself. Here for the first time is, as I think, the story of an ordinary person in the ordinary work-a-day world. Think of what fiction had been before it; either the picaresque novel bearing little relation to common experience—I have in my mind in English literature such things as Nashe's *Unfortunate Traveller*; or it had been the romance, deliberately not of the world, whether a philosophic treatise or a dainty toy; here, in English literature again, we can think of Sidney's *Arcadia* for the one, or Congreve's delightful *Incognita* for the other. After Defoe we get Richardson, Fielding, and so on, all of them writing studies of society; and I think the process is paralleled in other literatures. A generalization, we know, is always open to exceptions, and you, no doubt, will be able to think of more than I can inform you of. Yet I would maintain that on the whole this is true. Here, for the first time, in *Moll Flanders*, we have the unvarnished biography of a person you or I might meet in the street.

Or perhaps, but for God's grace, the biography of you or me. For although all Defoe's characters are outcasts, isolated in a hostile world, dissenters, if not in religion at least in morals, it is circumstance that forces them to the misdemeanours which exclude them. They are deformed by the pressure of society, by the fact that society encourages certain forms of evil. Thus Moll Flanders excuses her making herself out to be 'a fortune' so as to get a well-to-do husband by saying: 'This knowledge I soon learned by experience, viz. that the state of things was altered as to matrimony . . . that marriages were here the consequences of politic schemes for forming interests, and carrying on business, and that Love had no share, or but very little, in the matter.

'That as my sister-in-law at Colchester had said, beauty, wit, manners, sense, good-humour, education, virtue, piety or any other qualification, whether of body or mind, had no power to recommend; that money only made a woman agreeable; that men indeed chose mistresses by the gust of their affection . . . but for a wife no deformity would shock the fancy, no ill-qualities the judgment; the money was the thing; the portion was neither crooked nor monstrous, but the money was always agreeable, whatever the wife was.' Then follows some very good advice on how and why women should maintain their dignity, dictated to Moll by Defoe, the advocate of women's rights.

We follow her through her matrimonial or unsanctified adventures, in which ill-luck seems always to dog her steps; through her career as a pickpocket and thief, her transportation and her return; and here again Defoe's personal experience, his journalistic flair, his imaginative capacity for

E

piercing beneath the skin of other people, went to the making up of the creative writer. He knew all about Moll Flanders and her kind. Had he not lived five months in Newgate? Had he not himself experienced the pangs of the gaol-bird, and been able to study the inmost natures of these derelicts? Had he not ever since been close up against all the rapscallion elements of the population? If he could not be this person, who could? In fact he was: for here, possibly, more even than in any other of his books, Defoe succeeded in his marvellous, almost loving identification with the person he is describing. Just as Flaubert said, '*Madame Bovary, c'est moi*', so Defoe might have said, 'I am Moll Flanders'.

Why this old criminal is so entrancing is largely because of her supreme honesty *for the moment*. She lied in life, but she never lies to us. I would give in illustration the scene where all her maternal instincts swell up in a passionate lament of thwarted motherhood, on the occasion when she sees her American son after a lapse of many years, but is not permitted to disclose herself: ' . . . what yearnings of soul I had in me to embrace him, and weep over him; and how I thought all my entrails turned within me, that my very bowels moved, and I knew not what to do, as I know not now how to express those agonies. . . . I made as if I lay down to rest me . . . and lying on my face, wept, and kissed the ground that he had set his foot on.' She hadn't given this son a thought for over twenty years, had abandoned, we forget as we read how many other children to be left more or less as waifs and strays; yet we know that at this moment she felt as she says; there is no make-believe. Her instinct rises above experience, cancels her experience. What she tells us she felt at any given instant we know she did feel; what she says is of herself true, *for the moment*. Defoe, of course, leaves you to make the comment for yourself: he always does.

Here, for example, is an instance from *Roxana*. This 'fortunate mistress', compelled by circumstance to every ignoble action of her life, is now in Paris, where she hears that her first husband is to be found among the royal guard. She goes to see one of their companies march into the town, in the hope of discovering him. She describes the scene: ' . . . they indeed looked very gay, and as they marched very leisurely, I had time to take as critical a view, and make as nice a search among them as I pleased. Here, in a particular rank, eminent for one monstrous-sized man on the right, I say, I saw my gentleman again, and a very handsome jolly fellow he was, as any in the troop, though not so monstrous large as the great one I speak of, who, it seems, was, however, a gentleman of good family in Gascoigne, and was called the giant of Gascoigne. . . .' How circumstantial it all is! We know that Roxana must have been in Paris, and did actually see the troop march in. Yet note, the giant has nothing to do with the story: he is never mentioned again. But what a light this one mention throws upon the psychology of Roxana! a brilliant touch upon which I need not dilate.

One cannot help asking one's self on reflection—not at the time of reading, for then the question does not obtrude itself—how much was this subtle artistry of Defoe's unconscious? How much is the apparent artlessness really art? Can this hard-pressed, perpetually harassed, practical man of the world in truth be so simple-minded? It is either consummate artistry, or almost unbelievable innocence. It is only by this method of naïf truth-telling, we imagine, that he could have overcome the difficulties, the clumsiness, of the autobiographical form. Only so could his main characters be the finished analytical instruments that they are. They confess themselves to themselves, all unwittingly it seems, and so all the more revealingly to us. They burke nothing: Moll Flanders even tells us how she was tempted to murder the child she had robbed so as to be rid of a possible witness. Yet there must be art, for how else could Defore make a scene live as he does, not indeed a dramatic scene in the novelists' sense, but a *chose vue*? One asks one's

self whether the impeccable tact of omission from this sketch
of an incident during the plague could have been achieved
without a rigorous artistic discipline:

'The watchman had knocked at the door, it seems, when
he heard a great noise and crying, as above, and nobody
answered a great while, but at last one looked out and said,
with an angry quick tone, and yet a kind of crying voice, or a
voice of one that was crying, What d'ye want, that you make
such a knocking? He answered, I am the watchman, how do
you do? What is the matter? The person answered, What is
that to you? Stop the dead-cart. This, it seems, was about
one o'clock; soon after, as the fellow said, he stopped the
dead-cart, and then knocked again, but nobody answered; he
continued knocking, and the bell-man called out several
times, Bring out your dead; but nobody answered, till the man
that drove the cart being called to other houses, would stay no
longer, and drove away.'

Was Defoe aware of the atmosphere of stark horror, of the
sense of the macabre he was creating? It would seem unlikely. He appears to have turned to what we regard as intense creative writing as part of his journeyman's job: and this
spell of imaginative creation lasted only some five years. It is
outside his usual purely practical sphere—however much he
may have protested that this 'lying' as he chose to regard it,
was of immediate practical moral utility—as it is outside his
occult researches. It was not merely a question of leisure, for
even during the next seven years, when he wrote so many
purely journalistic articles, he employed his time, and earned
money, by writing books. But on what major works did he
employ this time? Why, on treatises concerning trade, or on
religion, or on the supernatural. There was *The Complete
English Tradesman*, of 450 pages (the first part of *Robinson
Crusoe* was only 364); there was *The Political History of the
Devil*, 408 pages; a work on useful discoveries and improve-
ments ran to over 300; another on morality in marriage

occupied over 400, while *A New Family Instructor* took up only about twenty less. There were books on street robberies and on Madagascar, on the reality of apparitions, on parochial tyranny, on the improvement of London. His pen never stopped; matter was never lacking in the well-stored repository of his mind; he seemed like a tireless machine. In his very last months some financial trouble revived his old persecution mania in aggravated form, and he died in hiding, at the end as isolated as any of his deathless characters. He passed away, to use the medical jargon of those days, in a lethargy, exhausted, we may think, by his immense labours.

In the last fifty years Defoe has very properly aroused much interest. Recently Mr. W. P. Trent in America, Professor Paul Dottin in Toulouse, and lastly Professor J. R. Sutherland in London, have done most valuable exploratory, and most illuminating, critical work. Admirers of Defoe must be deeply indebted to them—as I myself so obviously am—but there will always be exploratory and critical work to do where Defoe is concerned. It is a measure of his genius. His life is so full of mysteries, his writing so multifarious, that we shall never be satisfied that we know and understand all. He will always be fascinating and he will always be attractive: fascinating because the struggle between the moralist and the artist never fails to produce delighted surprise in the reader; attractive because his writing remains fresh, his pictures amazingly vivid, his touch on so many sides of human emotion so beautifully sure. Some fifteen years ago we observed the bicentenary of his death: in some fifteen years more we shall perhaps celebrate the tercentenary of his birth. He, no doubt, would wish us to remember the moralist: we, most likely shall salute the artist.

JOSEPH ADDISON

*The Spectator**

'La sagesse! quel thème inépuisable!'—*Amiel*

ADDISON'S period of enforced political idleness was not given over only to such occasions, for he was chiefly engaged upon the work whereon his fame most firmly rests, journalistic essay writing.

In 1709, bettering a method initiated by Defoe, Steele launched *The Tatler*, of which the name was chosen in compliment to the Fair Sex. The sheets were sent to Dublin, whence Addison, guessing by an allusion in one of them that their author was his friend, at once began to contribute. It was the very thing for him; there, without fear of exposure, he could try his hand. It was, as Miss Aikin said, 'what his diffidence required, a safe and private channel'. If he failed, the papers need never be known to be his; if he succeeded, he could in course of time step forward to take the honours due. In any case, modesty apart, it was a wise precaution to be anonymous, for the expression of views might be attended by uncomfortable results: bread cast upon calm waters might return in an unpleasant form after many days, when the waters were stormy. But in such a journal as *The Tatler* Addison really could express himself—and did, with the result

* Reprinted from *Essays in Biography 1680–1726*, Oxford University Press, 1925.

that nothing reveals him more clearly than the long series of essays he wrote for various periodicals.

Of course absolute concealment over a great stretch of time could not be hoped for, but there would always be a doubt as to who had written any particular paper. And here Steele, with his lamentable recklessness, came in useful. He was the ideal collaborator; he served as whipping-boy, a happy state of affairs not unobserved by Gay. 'I have thought', he wrote of Steele and Addison, 'that the conjunction of those two great geniuses (who seem to stand in a class by themselves, so high above all other wits), resembles that of two famous statesmen [Somers and Halifax] in a late reign . . . the first was continually at work behind the curtain; drew up and pre-pared all the schemes and designs which the latter still drove on, and stood out exposed to the world, to receive its praise or censures.'[1]

Indeed, left by himself, Addison had not the nerve to 'drive on' a journal, and his attempt to set up *The Whig Ex-aminer* in 1710 proved a failure, though to be sure political polemics were not his *forte*. If Somers and Halifax had reared him for this, they made a mistake in the subject they chose for training, for in that field he was no match for Prior, whom they had foolishly allowed to secede. Addison's *Whig Examiner*s have, as Macaulay said, 'as little merit as anything that he wrote',[2] and in December, after eight numbers, hearing that Swift was to take over *The Examiner*, the Tory instrument, he 'avoided the contest as at once doubtful, harassing and in-vidious'.[3]

At about this time Steele abruptly ended *The Tatler*, not that it was beginning to be thought dull, except by Swift, but that one or two opinions too Whiggish for the ruling powers had made certain difficulties. It was impossible to keep Steele's pen out of the political inkpot. But the venture had been so successful, so much to Addison's taste, that the friends almost

---

[1] *Present State of Wit.*   [2] Macaulay MS.   [3] Scott, 112.

at once started another journal: but this time it was Addison who decided on the tone. This paper would be on the same lines as *The Tatler*—less the news items—but would go at once farther and more carefully, while Steele was firmly kept in check. This journal would have as author a 'man' who was strictly impartial, observing 'an exact neutrality between Whigs and Tories',[1] in fact a mere Spectator commenting with perfect aloofness, and never risking the loss of his ears, like Defoe—for no one else under such conditions could stand 'unabashed on high'. Far from being a party organ, it would direct men's minds away from faction, thus seconding the efforts of the Royal Society, which, as everybody knew, had with its 'air-pump, barometer, quadrant' and the like fal-de-lals, been founded for that very purpose.[2] It would deal particularly with those seemingly trivial, but in reality grave errors incident to mankind living in society, and would 'endeavour to enliven morality with wit and to temper wit with morality'. 'But there are none', Mr. Spectator promised, 'to whom this paper will be more useful than to the female world.'[3]

To some this might seem a small conception; but in Addison's hand its scope was well-nigh limitless. 'It was said of Socrates', he wrote, 'that he brought philosophy down from heaven, to inhabit among men; and I shall be ambitious to have it said of me, that I have brought philosophy out of closets and libraries, schools and colleges, to dwell in clubs and assemblies, at tea-tables and coffee-houses.'[4]

Philosophy! It has a fine sound; but what sort of philosophy is it that can flourish when 'punctually served up as part of the tea-equipage'? Did George Berkeley smile a little when he read the passage, and think of Locke, Spinoza, and his other adversaries? But it was at once clear that Mr. Spectator had not the least design of tackling those problems which are

[1] *Spectator*, 1: 1 March, 1711.   [2] *Spectator*, 262.
[3] *Spectator*, 10.   [4] *Spectator*, 10.

the brute material of philosophy, of dealing with those puzzling questions of reality, or of the validity of the ego. Not for him the pleasure and the pride of categories, nor the airy stilts of abstraction. Rather was the British Virgil about to become the suave and homely Marcus Aurelius of the tea-tables; and it soon appeared that his notion of philosophy was the elegant common sense apt to mould man into the *parfait honnête homme* dear to that very French society he paradoxically so much despised. Nay, it was something even more gentle. Nothing was too little for it—not the wearing of patches, the use of rings, the frivolity of the Gallic race, the exact degree of volubility proper to educated persons. The journal became a manual of deportment; and a statue of philosophy as con-ceived by Mr. Spectator might represent a benign grand-mother knitting by the fireside, occasionally casting a slightly severe glance over her spectacles. And the old lady's more familiar name would be Common Sense.

Common sense! It was the dawn of the century that prided itself upon its mastery of it. But the principle is a negative one, the words capable of many interpretations. Yet Addison might have appealed to Berkeley for confirmation of his doctrine that common sense was the basis of philosophy, a thesis the latter was then writing his Dialogues to prove. 'You see, Hylas,' Philonous perorates, 'the water of yonder fountain, how it is forced upwards, in a round column, to a certain height; at which it breaks, and falls back into the basin from whence it rose: its ascent as well as descent proceeding from the same uniform law or principle of *gravitation*. Just so, the same principles which, at first view, lead to Scepticism, pursued to a certain point, bring men back to Common Sense.'

But what seems common sense to one man is often un-common nonsense to another. 'Coxcombs vanquished Berkeley with a grin', and Sir Roger de Coverley would no doubt have refuted the Irishman's peculiar form of that commodity by stamping particularly hard upon the ground. It was Dr.

Johnson's method. But there was another kind of philosophy to help Mr. Spectator, that which caused La Bruyère to say that 'on ne doit écrire que pour l'instruction ... pour le changement des mœurs et la réformation de ceux qui lisent'—a view dear to Ruskin and Trollope, but which was unintelligible to Dryden, hard as he tried to assimilate it in his last years. So Mr. Spectator banished doubts; he pinned his faith to La Bruyère, and calling his work 'philosophy', proceeded to inculcate into the fair sex those precepts which, if followed, would make its members the most useful and agreeable of man's domestic animals.

'An ingenious man', so Sir Charles Grandison referred to Addison;[1] 'an ingenious man, to whose works your sex, and if *yours ours*, are more obliged than to those of any single man in the British world.' If yours, ours, there's the crux. For woman was to be the better half of man in that she was to give infinitely less trouble. She was to be intelligent, but not too clever, good-tempered, and docile to opinion; without opinion, in fact, for nothing was worse for a face than party zeal.[2] If married, not only was she to give no cause for jealousy, she was to feel none:[3] in short, if the home was not happy, it was to be entirely her fault, never the man's. Addison's ideal was to create the Victorian helpmeet, one who could write to her husband, 'my own love, I will trust you. You will succeed, and I am patient. Your little wife knows you will not lose an opportunity which may lead to success, and if you are unfortunate she is there to kiss away all disappointment, and to console you as well as she can.'[4] Addison, in fact, looking back in horror upon Restoration days and that monstrous regiment of women, was fitting the female neck for the virile yoke, and Henry Esmond had no illusions as to the design. 'There's not a writer of my time of any note', he protested, 'with the exception of poor Dick Steele, that does not speak of a woman

---

[1] *Grandison,* ii, Letter 27.   [2] *Spectator,* 57.   [3] *Spectator,* 171.
[4] The first Lady Esher to her husband. *Esher Letters.*

as of a slave, and scorn and use her as such. Mr. Pope, Mr. Congreve, Mr. Addison, Mr. Gay, every one of 'em, sing in this key, each according to his nature and politeness.'[1]

And between them they succeeded in creating the women they wished, a long line through the Jane Bennets to the Amelia Sedleys—they and the age which was tired of the Lady Betty Modishes and the Hoyden Clumseys, who seem to have displaced the Dorothy Osbornes as well as the Barbara Palmers and Olivia Vernishes. Certainly these 'writers of note' set the fashion for the eighteenth century. If any one cares to look up Squire Western's opinions of the charms and sphere of women, he will find them, though phrased differently, identical with Addison's—and, strangely enough, with Squire Allworthy's. Addison, it is true, would not have spoken to his daughter as Western did to Sophy, but it is probable that had occasion arisen he would have acted towards her precisely as Mr. Harlowe did to Clarissa. In this matter, as in many others, he rightly interpreted the views of his contemporaries.

It is unlikely, of course, that Sarah Marlborough, or Marlborough's Misses, or Mrs. de la Rivière Manley, the unscrupulous pamphleteer, paid any heed to such hortations; and one wonders what bold Lady Mary Pierpoint thought of them as she made her runaway match with Addison's grave and didactic friend Mr. Wortley Montagu. But other members of the fair sex seemed to dote on *The Spectator*. They read it eagerly. It adorned three thousand tea-tables, and so universal was their suffrage, that Tickell, writing verses 'To the Supposed Author of *The Spectator*', crooned:

> Received by thee, I prophesy my rhymes
> The praise of virgins in succeeding times;

a curious compliment to a man who in the same poem was, as usual, referred to as the British Virgil, while 'Fame, Heav'n and Hell' were his 'exalted theme'.

It is true, they were. But 'the middle way is best', and these

[1] *Esmond*, I. xii.

exalted themes were treated in that spirit of the golden medio-
crity that is the only really safe guide either in the conduct of
daily life or the promptings of the spirit. Addison did not care
for Icarian flights of speculative thought, or for those emotions,
so heavily paid for, plucked in the dark forests of the soul.
Was not the 'artificial wildness' of Fontainebleau more welcome
than the terrifying abysses of the Alps? Thus the thoughts that
he developed in his modulated phrases seemed to many
exactly the things they also were thinking, and indeed, his
moral precepts were bound to meet with acquiescence in a
post-Collier age which blossomed into Societies for the Reformation of Manners. In effect, *The Tatler* and *The Spectator*
did not lead public opinion, they expressed it; they helped it to
make up its mind. If, for instance, it was beginning to be felt
that lap-dogs were becoming a nuisance, Isaac Bickerstaff
would deluge them with whimsical scorn; but where public
opinion gave no sign that venerable gentleman was silent.
Petticoats might be judged too wide, bonnets too high; but
since no one suggested that hanging youths for trivial offences
was abominable, not the airiest breath of ridicule was wafted
upon this barbarism from the club that contained Sir Roger de
Coverley, Sir Andrew Freeport, and Will Honeycomb. *Vox
populi, vox Dei;* and it was through the voice of the people
that Addison hearkened to the voice of God. He had stumbled
upon the secret of successful journalism.

Originality, alas! was out of the question, for mankind had
reached the farthest stretch of wisdom. 'We have little left us,
but to represent the common sense of mankind in more
strong, more beautiful, or more uncommon lights.'[1] Boileau
had said it: Horace had proved it. This being the case, Addison could never shock, for it is the new view that most re-
volts mankind. 'The novelty, Philonous, the novelty! There's
the danger.' Thus in his 'visions' he could deal with 'exalted
themes' in a way that must appeal to every one. Not a virgin

[1] *Spectator,* 253.

but could appreciate *The Vision of Mirza*, that simple allegory of life and death and future reward. It might be objected that such a theme was perilously close to religion, that such a subject if any might conceal a trap. But there, as in politics, Addison picked his way gingerly, offending none. Was it not admitted that 'there is not a more melancholy object than a man who has his head turned with religious enthusiasm'?[1] Naturally he rejected superstition, not, however, on the grounds of hated science,[2] but on the solid basis of a simple faith he had no difficulty in believing. For he was never borne upward very far in the fountain of Philonous, and even a constant study of Bayle's Dictionary failed to undermine the thoughts he had imbibed in the Deanery at Lichfield.

His literary criticism, too, guided the steps of his readers into paths they were willing to tread. Written not in the spirit of Dryden's prefaces or of Pope's *Essay on Criticism*, it pointed out the spiritual rather than the literary beauties of Milton, as it did the simple feeling of 'Chevy Chase'. And, though resting on authority, it is not surprising that Dr. Johnson found him a poor critic, though for the wrong reasons, and that Landor preferred the judgments of Steele, for Addison was not a critic so much as a popularizer, the forebear of a manifold line. His dissertations too were so written that it needed little thought to follow them, indeed only so much as might conveniently be spared in the coffee-houses of the busy world.

Nevertheless popularity is not gained merely by dubbing oneself 'censor of manners' and uttering comfortable commonplaces, by preaching the sweet doctrine of the obvious virtues—politeness; honesty, political and commercial; continence—lest disfigurement follow; truth-telling, faith, charity; and above all, prudence, respect for opinion. The public of Queen Anne's day read *The Spectator*, not because it was pious, but because it was charmingly, and on the whole freely, written. It might sometimes become a little tedious, but that

---

[1] *Spectator*, 201.   [2] See *Tatlers*, 216, 221.

was only to be expected, since Addison chose to write over the
initials C.L.I.O., and the muse of that name is, as we know,
'apt to be pompous'. On the other hand it was full of pleasant
little tales from the classics, or from Bayle's Dictionary, and
miniatures of character such as would have delighted La
Bruyère. Wit enlivened morality; and the fair sex, while no
doubt feeling virtuously in agreement with a man who hated
fashion as much as any mid-Victorian, could hold their sides
with laughter at reading that one of the honorific titles of the
Shah of Persia was 'nutmeg of delight'. For though Addison
'would not willingly laugh but in order to instruct',[1] he was a
master in the art of gentle humour. Indeed, had not his goal
been the ears of the fair sex, it might be supposed his humour
was too gentle.

In any case the even flow of his prose was most seductive to
the circles that would only read that which could easily be read.
His English lies liquid on the palate like a really happy port—
but it is a ladies' port. For in his writing there is none of the
rhythmed bell-note of Browne, the rolling swell of Milton's
cadence, nor the vigorous thud of Dryden's galloping hoofs.
Beside Swift's rapier the edge is waxy; compared with Bolingbroke's delicate architecture Addison's is—Addison Road.
But, still more to jostle metaphor, his readers could, as it were,
feel themselves deliciously rocked on phrases that swing like
cockle-boats in the wake of a great ship. His prose, in short,
like his precepts, is, in the Johnsonian phrase, 'the model of the
middle style'.

To the student of drum-and-trumpet history, or to those
whose interest lies in disentangling clear lines of development in the chaos of human strife, *The Spectator* must seem a
singular growth in the hot-bed of faction presented by the last
four years of Queen Anne's reign. Statesmen, soldiers, even
bishops, appeared in the smithy of double-handed intrigue,
dangerous with white-hot sparks, in which, not without

[1] *Spectator*, 179.

many slain, the British Constitution was hazardously and blindly forged. Then paper and ink were barbed weapons that might easily wound the many hands that wielded them, and often did. In an atmosphere of Guiscard attempts, crowds flocking to see the body of Harley's would-be murderer suspended in a window; of bandbox plots which brought so much ridicule on courageous Dr. Swift; amid rumours of attempted landings by the Chevalier St. George, the king over the water; or gripping fears as to the Queen's health; surrounded by tempers that could pass the Tory Occasional Conformity and Schism Acts and plan the Whig procession Steele was to lead;[1] when men who had not forgotten William's usurpation or the Monmouth rebellion anxiously saw to their fire-arms, and Mohocks struck terror into astrologers, it seems incredible that men should have had time to read *The Spectator*. But however stirring revolutions may be, for the most part of the time the normal life goes on—since it is that by which we live—and men pursue their favourite callings. We may remember that in 1712 the Royal Society published its vindication of Newton against Leibnitz as the inventor of the Infinitesimal Calculus, that Collins and the Arian Clarke continued their metaphysical discussions of other-worldly matters, that Berkeley composed his dialogues, Lord Mohun killed the Duke of Hamilton in a duel, and Pope took lessons in painting.

Thus through all the geyser-spouting of pamphlets and libels engendered by the ballad-breeding—and Peer-creating— Peace of Utrecht; in the midst of fierce criticism such as that contained in *The Conduct of the Allies;* in a thundery air of suppression, vituperation, calumny, and Grub Street taxes, Addison and his little senate were able calmly to write *The Spectator*, which Swift might find boring[2]—he believed they were 'prettily written'—but which circles of young ladies found diverting, and breakfast-tables an excuse for silence.

[1] See *Essays in Bibliography*, p. 136.
[2] Swift to Stella, 18 Nov. 1711: 'Do you read the *Spectators*? I never do.'

Yet it was indeed a staggering performance in that there was nothing 'party' about it; that is, it could not deal with subjects which at that crisis of the nation's history were the only ones of acute public interest. Non-party, when the safety of the new, hard-won régime called loudly for the fierce trying-out of opposite views! But that was just its secret. It could please Stella in Dublin, or make good bundles for maternal devotion to send to Lord Raby in Holland: and being a comment on the things of the day that did not in the least matter, it brought profit without fear to the writers and the printer. It was so eminently safe that one could hardly refuse to subscribe. If it did not cause excitement like *The Public Spirit of the Whigs*, nor raise laughter so boisterous as the account of Prior's journey into France, it was, on the other hand, as suitable to the antechamber of Lord Halifax as to the boudoir of Lady Masham. Bolingbroke and Marlborough might not waste their time over it, but Drs. Arbuthnot and Garth might without a second thought approvingly con the same passages of dramatic criticism, or smile at the same material version of a psalm. It shone alike upon the just and the unjust. Like a 'whimsical Tory' it seemed at once to be against war and against Jacobitism; like an occasional conformer it could compound with conscience for the sake of doing good.

It is all the same obvious that a journal like *The Spectator*, with the work falling chiefly on one man, cannot go on for ever. Polished work is not done offhand, and although Addison could dictate almost the finished essay once he had it clear in his head, he nevertheless polished considerably. Nor is elaborate and considered description, if it is not quite criticism, such as he wrote on *Paradise Lost*, lightly thrown off. Moreover, even perfect wisdom is not really inexhaustible, nor can any man pontificate urbanely for every morning's breakfast without reaching a limit, although the subject be the sum total of the universe. Universality itself begins to appear a trifle ridiculous, it becomes too much, in Corbière's phrase, a 'mélange adultère de tout', and *The Spectator* did not elude carpers.

Indeed, there was something about the Apollonian calm of Mr. Spectator, with his curt but superior statements that he would not answer critical fools,[1] that must have acted as a goad to such writers as the author of *The British Censor*, a not un-amusing, nor wholly unjust pamphlet in verse which appeared towards the end of 1712. After jibing at Mr. Spectator for praising 'Chevy Chase' *because* many parallel passages can be found in Virgil—which was not altogether fair since this criticism had been forestalled—it went on to describe the activities of the Censor:

> All Things by Thee are clearly Understood
> From *Homer* to the *Children in the Wood*.
> Maxims of Schools, and the grave Ayrs of France,
> Ethics and Modes, Divinity and Dance;
> Pain, Bliss, Hate, Friendship, Lamentation, Song,
> To thy extended Province, all belong;
> But Poetry is thy peculiar Care,
> And here thy Judgment is . . . beyond Compare.
> Thro' thy just Praise each arch Pretender shines
> With *Blackmore*'s easie, clear, and nervous lines . . .

So far good; the reference to Blackmore's voluminous tur-gidity is excellent; but now the verses tend to become personal:

> But Tickell is, (thy Theame's Sublimer Scope)
> Of ev'ry Muse, and Grace the springing Hope,
> Tickell, (surprizing Object of thy Love!)
> Who do's the just reverse of *Denham* prove,
> (Deep, yet not clear, not gentle and yet dull,
> Raging, yet weak, o'erflowing, yet not full;)[2]

Such criticism contained some things too near the truth to be

---

[1] *Spectator*, 355.

[2] *Censor*. The forgetful reader may like to be reminded that Denham's lines on the Thames, expressing his aim in poetry, run:

> Though deep, yet clear; though gentle, yet not dull;
> Strong without rage, without o'erflowing full.

F

ignored, and if at all common, it was evidently time for Mr. Spectator 'to go off the stage', as he said. Thus on the 6th December, 1712 a number, signed by Steele in full, announced the cessation of the journal, acknowledgments being made by name of all the contributors—except one. This gentleman, while being given the place of honour, thanked with exceeding generosity for his work on *The Spectator* and *Tatler*, and for help in *The Tender Husband*, as well as being made the subject of reverend and friendly compliment, remained modestly veiled behind the discreet pseudonym of C.L.I.O.

LAURENCE STERNE*

AN author whose books we read again—and where Sterne is
concerned—again and again—is one who continually en-
tertains, enlivens, makes us not so much think as be, be more
alertly than is normal in our humdrum daily life. There are,
admittedly, various levels of being. That we experience from
reading Plato or Berkeley, or for that matter *Gulliver's Travels*,
is not that we more easily attain by reviewing at intervals our
knowledge of *The Newcomes*, or, at a less actual level, *Huckle-
berry Finn*, for fiction operates on different centres of being
from those approached by philosophy. What we seek in fiction
is a realization of ourselves not as (possibly) immortal beings
but as people living here and now amid neighbours who are
'such creatures as we are, in such a world as the present one',
who we would wish to understand, like, and, no doubt, for
such is human nature, judge.

Whether consciously or not, we ask to be talked to on a
conversational level, highly intelligent, of course (though this
does nor preclude gossip). This is where Sterne scores so
heavily. 'Writing', Tristam Shandy declared, 'when properly
managed (as you may be sure I think mine is) is but a different
name for conversation.' And how diverse the conversation is,
ranging from placket-holes to Locke, from the early Church
fathers or the military engineer Stevinus to the somewhat
clumsy obstetrics of Dr. Slop, always enchantingly about Mr.
and Mrs. Shandy, or the ever-lovable Uncle Toby and his
temerarious advances upon the fortress, not too sternly

* This article first appeared in *The Times Literary Supplement*, 8 June, 1962 and
is reprinted by kind permission of the Editor.

defended, of the Widow Wadman, and, naturally, Yorick himself. And what of Eugenius and Corporal Trim? If you do not enjoy *Tristam Shandy* you are not worthy to read *Twelfth Night;* if *A Sentimental Journey* makes no appeal to you, it were as well for you to avoid *Love's Labour's Lost;* or, in another realm, if the Sermons of Yorick seem to you flat and unprofitable—they are 'aimed point-blank'—you will waste your time in reading those of Joseph Butler.

The more discussion there is about Sterne, either as a man or as a writer, the more there seems to be to discuss, as M. Henri Fluchère's *Laurence Sterne: De l'homme à l'oeuvre* exemplifies. The first theme would seem to be that of his sentimentality, a word about which there is some disagreement. Mr. Eliot has defined sentimentality as 'emotion in excess of the facts', but who is to judge of that? It might be better to define it as 'the emotion someone else feels that you don't happen to share'. No doubt there are some things upon which most of us will agree. It is sentimental, we will say, to blubber over a dead donkey (not that Sterne did, in spite of the notorious accusation), but we may doubt whether it is so to remember that sympathetic glance, that tremendous sunset, that moment of shared danger or shared delight. Where do we draw the line between sensibility, sentiment and sentimentality?

Sterne, we realize, lived in the period which saw the birth of 'sentiment', leading to Mackenzie's *The Man of Feeling* and a torrent of handkerchief-wetting fiction admirably described by Dr. J. M. S. Tompkins in her at once appreciative and duly derisory *The Popular Novel in England, 1776-1866*. But how far do we get in our assessment of Sterne in belabouring him as the apostle of sentimentality? There may have been something in the cult of the idea that justified Chesterfield's unprintable derivation of the word, yet after all, the contributor to *The Critical Review* of January, 1782, quoted by M. Fluchère, was surely in the right of it when, commenting upon the tear that the Recording Angel dropped upon Uncle Toby's oath, blotting it out for ever, he asserted that it 'is a conceit, but a conceit of genius, glowing with the warmth of a heart truly sentimental'.

But still it is hazardous to draw the line between 'the man of feeling' and the glutton of sentiment. Sterne, very much in the current of the humanitarian movement that began in the middle of the century, perhaps overdid the captive starling, the belaboured ass, and Maria of Moulines. Yet we sometimes suspect that he was humorously in control of his sentimentality. When seeking the tomb of Amandus and Amanda to drop a tributary tear upon it, and finding there was none, he could say: 'What would I have given for my uncle *Toby*, to have whistled Lillo bullero!' In what we can honourably call sentiment, that is, a deep sympathy with most of his fellow-creatures, he did not always put on the brake. And who would wish it? Who would want the story of Le Fever altered by the veriest jot? Yet his affectionate portraits of the characters, from Uncle Toby to Obadiah, are all painted with a touch, or more, of humour—after all, the best of creatures can be a little absurd—though without the faintest trace of malice. Even when he discourses upon Walter Shandy's handbook for the education of Tristram, the *Tristra-paedia*, it is with an appreciative chuckle, and without that aloofness, mark of the comic spirit, with which Sir Austin Feverel's 'System' for Richard is treated by a master in that mode.

You always know where you are with Sterne, though you never know where you will be the next minute. From Yorick's statement that a good sermon should come from the heart and not from the head, you are diverted to Phutatorius's unlucky adventure with the hot chestnut; an argument with a French commissary brings you up against the most baffling of metaphysical questions:

My good friend, quoth I..as sure as I am I—and you are you—

And who are you? said he—Don't puzzle me; said I.

We get touching stories and events, and also magnificently
absurd ones, such as that of Slawkenbergius and his monstrous nose, or that of the Abbess of Andouillets, who by
splitting with a nun the swearword necessary to make their
horse go forward, cleared it of all sin. But within all the tales,
as well as throughout the main tale, there is an extraordinarily
wide range of themes: the medical ideas of the day—radical
heat and radical moisture—scholastic theology, fortification,
starry 'influences' such as interested Nicolas Culpeper, the
relation of hobby-horses to character, or of wit and judgment: the complete catalogue would be pages long, and
there is no guessing what theme will come up next.

This jumping-aboutness, we might call it, is made possible
by the form, or, if you like, the formlessness of *Tristam
Shandy*, in which Sterne deliberately defied all rules, even those
of Horace, as he is careful to say. Time, progress in time,
means nothing to him, and since there is no story, except
possibly that of Uncle Toby's amours, there is no reason why
it should. What he wants to write is 'the history of what
passes in a man's own mind'. This takes him backward as
memory and association lead him, and enables him to be in
several places at once:

> I am at this moment walking across the market-place of
> *Auxerre* with my father and my uncle *Toby*, in our way back to
> dinner—and I am this moment also entering *Lyons* with my
> post-chaise broke into a thousand pieces—and I am moreover
> this moment in a handsome pavilion built by *Pringello* upon the
> banks of the *Garonne*. . . .

So much for the time-space continuum, as we used to say
a few years ago. As Tristam Shandy put it:

> . . . the machinery of my work is of a species by itself; two
> contrary motions are introduced into it, and reconciled, which
> were thought to be at variance with each other. In a word, my
> work is digressive, and it is progressive too—and at the same
> time.

Moreover, the two movements have been 'so complicated and
involved . . . that the whole machine has been kept a-going'.
M. Fluchère puts all this more vividly, using what in our
jargon we would call 'contemporary' (meaning up-to-date)
terms, and, we might think, more illuminatingly than Sterne
did himself. Speaking of the multitude of ideas, and the so-
called disorder of the work, he declares:

> Il semble donc que nous assisitions à un bombardement molé-
> culaire d'idées, qui se déclanche par chaînes, s'interrompt et
> repart dans une direction imprévue, traversé tout à coup par
> une irruption latérale ou connexe, qui, à son tour, déclanchera
> une nouvelle série.

But how far Sterne was deliberately structural must remain a
matter of conjecture. It is enough that we can find in his work
such structure as we can make out of our individual lives, if we
are honest enough to know them.

Continually interspersed with the molecules with which we
are bombarded are those charged with nuclei destructive of all
pretentiousness and pedantry, such as the well-known:

> Of all the cants that are canted in this canting world—though
> the cant of hypocrites may be the worst—the cant of criticism
> is the most tormenting!

So much for Smelfungus, and all his ilk; but what of Mrs.
Grundy? Sterne tilts continually, some may think too much so,
at prudery; and in discussing him one cannot evade the question
of his 'indecorum', to use a decorous word. This banned
Tristram Shandy and *A Sentimental Journey* from the drawing-
room tables of Mrs. Montagu and other blue-stockings, as
Mr. Alan B. Howes showed in his investigatory *Yorick and the
Critics*. It is, let us confess it frankly, enormous fun. There is
no vice in it; it is merely a recognition of normal human impulses. When Sterne told an interlocutor, 'Madam; my book is
like that infant playing on the floor: he often shows what is

usually concealed, but all with the utmost innocence', he was playing the game it so hugely amused him to play. For the fun in his improper passages lies in his catching you out. If you think them improper, that is your fault, not his; the onus is entirely on you.

> —Here are two senses, cried *Eugenius*, as we walk'd along, pointing with the forefinger of his right hand to the word *Crevice*, in the one hundred and seventy-eighth page of the first volume of this book of books;—and here are two senses— quoth he—And here are two roads, replied I, turning short upon him—a dirty and a clean one—which shall we take?— The clean, by all means, replied *Eugenius*. *Eugenius*, said I, stepping before him, and laying my hand upon his breast—to define—is to distrust.—Thus I triumph'd over *Eugenius*; but I triumph'd over him as I always do, like a fool.—'Tis my comfort, however, I am not an obstinate one; therefore. . . .

And Sterne proceeds to define 'a nose'. There again we may be apt to miss one of the points, since, in one edition at any rate, the caption at the side of the page reads: 'To define is to distrust'. You may have been caught out by the episode of the *fille de chambre* in *A Sentimental Journey*, and you may take the wrong road in its final chapter 'The Case of Delicacy'; but if you do so, it is entirely your fault, not Yorick's. Did he not all along, as he said, depend upon the cleanliness of his readers' imaginations?

NATURE POETRY in the EARLY EIGHTEENTH CENTURY*

A QUESTION that will raise in the minds of many readers will be: 'What do you mean by "nature"?' That is a simpler question to answer than: 'What did the men of the eighteenth century mean by the term?' That, as we know, is an extremely complex affair, having been told that they meant at least seventeen things. However, what I mean primarily in this context, is simply what you and I and the man and woman next door mean by it in ordinary conversation, what we might call the tangible and visible things around us which are not man-made; the world and the things that grow on it, the creatures (excluding man) that live in it: also, in response to what the poets of that time wrote about, a wider sweep, from microbes to the galactic system.

In his *Preface to Eighteenth Century Poetry*, Professor Sutherland recalls a remark of Stopford Brooke's, that 'When Pope was writing, the love of Nature for itself had quite decayed'. Similarly, Logie Robertson confidently told his readers that 'Thomson's great merit lies in his restoration of nature to the domain of poetry from which it had been banished by Pope and his school'. We, of course, know that such statements are 'wildly wrong'; they stagger us, both as regards people in general and Pope in particular. Yet those writers were intelligent men and considerable scholars: they must have meant something, and it may be helpful to guess what they implied.

* Reprinted from *Essays and Studies, 1965* published for The English Association by John Murray (Publishers) Ltd., and reprinted by Wm. Dawson and Sons Ltd.

The state of affairs seems to have been this: the late Victorians
—if one may include those two scholars among them—being
other than the Augustans, children of a later heritage, looked
at different things in nature, or, if they looked at the same
things, did so with eyes differently focused. Secondly, they
sought another kind of stimulus; thirdly they expected nature,
nature as they observed it, to contain implications foreign to
the Augustan apprehensions; and, finally, they were ac-
customed to a certain kind of imagery. Finding Augustan
nature poetry disappointing in these respects, they turned their
attention from it, and came to the conclusion that it did not
exist.

Most of us, of course, in any age, tend to respond strongly
only to poetry in which we find what we expect to find. And
we know, even from what has happened in this century, how
rapidly our expectations change, how quickly one fashion
displaces another. We are filled of one kind of poetic or imaginative nourishment, and crave a different *pabulum;* yet do we
not make a mistake if we think that any poetry that once had
the suffrage of a generation can mean nothing to us now? We
have, to be sure, to co-operate: and to understand, and so
enjoy and be refreshed by the poetry of a previous age, we are
not only have to recognize our common humanity, but also
accept the idiom of that age.

So here my concern will be, not to take *seriatim* the points
mentioned above, but to try to realize the impact of 'nature' on
the minds and emotions of the men and women who wrote, if
not always poetry, at least verse, and of those who read it. I
would wish to present, so far as I can, as much by implication as by statement, by illustration rather than by argument,
what the writers of those days made of the various possible
reactions to the immediately apprehensible world, and to the
world which it needed not only perception to register but also
imagination to penetrate.

To begin with the simplest, which is also the earliest form, with what we might call 'homely' poetry. What was the impulse that lay behind the writings of such poems as, say, Pomfret's *The Choice* (1700), or King's *Mully of Mountown* (1704)? We note, naturally, that people in those days did not need a great head of what we have come to call 'poetic pressure' to write verse. The form was to a large extent vulgarly popular, and almost as common a medium of chatting, shall we call it, as letter-writing. What is perhaps the most famous poem of this kind, Matthew Green's *The Spleen* (1737), was actually dubbed 'An Epistle', though the term 'epistle', to be sure, covered a multitude of utterances at various levels of intensity.

This poetry was evidently in part a harking back to Horace, genial exercises in the 'retirement' theme; Parnell, for example, in his poem *Health* (1714), declared that 'Tully's Tusculum' revived in his. This further involved the theme of solitude, which can no more than be touched on here. But though these things might be in the background of the writers, what we find expressed in this homely poetry is the sense of pleasure at living among country sights and sounds—though by no means cut off from society. We might call it 'country poetry' rather than 'nature poetry', typified by Pomfret's

> Near some fair Town I'd have a private Seat,
> Built uniform, not Little, nor too Great;
> Better, if on a Rising Ground it stood;
> Fields on this side, on that a Neighb'ring Wood.
> It should within no other Things contain,
> But what are useful, necessary, plain. . . .
> A little Garden, Grateful to the Eye;
> And a cool Rivulet run murm'ring by;
> On whose delicious Banks a stately Row
> Of Shady Limes, or Sycamores, shou'd grow.

That is a direct, if not very violent reaction. Pomfret, a country parson, is just telling what he enjoys. He is not, as most of the poets were to do, extracting a moral from the scene (no sermons in stones for him!), nor expecting the scene to suggest one, as Lady Winchilsea does in her *Petition for an Absolute Retreat* (1713):

> Thus from crowds and noise remov'd,
> Let each moment be improv'd;
> Every object still produce
> Thoughts of pleasure and of use.
> When some river slides away
> To increase the boundless sea,
> Think we then how time does haste
> To grow eternity at last. . . .

Retreat from cares, yes, from a life involving obligations, but not always for thinking; sometimes for grosser reasons, as with William King who does not climb very high up Parnassus:

> Mountown! thou sweet retreat from Dublin cares,
>   [which he did not allow to pester him unduly]
> Be famous for thy apples and thy pears,
> For turnips, carrots, lettuce, beans and pease;
> For Peggy's butter and for Peggy's cheese.
> May clouds of pigeons round about thee fly!
> But sometimes condescend to make a pye.
> May fat geese gaggle. . . .

and so on, with gastronomic relish proper to the author-to-be of *The Art of Cookery* (1708). He, it may be thought, is unduly explicit, in contrast with Walsh, who in *The Retirement* (1692) is far more general, we might even say perfunctory, dismissing the country in two lines:

> All hail, ye fields, where constant peace attends;
> All hail, ye sacred solitary groves.

No detail. It would appear that in the early eighteenth century a clear reference to nature was enough to arouse a complex of responses: the setting was given, and the reader was expected to fill in the details with whatever attendant delights he might associate with them. It was only courteous; the reader was supposed to have some experience of his own. We need, perhaps, to remind ourselves that after all in those days, though society was tending to be urban, most people lived in the country, and did not need to be told about it. Country towns were what we would now call large villages, London itself no larger than a country town of today, with what we now call the suburbs objectives of longish country walks.

And what beguiled the men of those days, and therefore the versifiers, was not only the peace of the visible countryside, but what went on in the country, among beasts and birds and insects—and indeed among men, from Gay's *Rural Sports* (1713) to Somerville's *The Chace* (1735): but the goings-on of man may be left aside here, though they are seldom absent from the nature poetry of the time. With the creatures we get a much greater particularity, as we can see by looking for a moment at that very pleasant, to some extent utilitarian Georgic *Cyder* (1708) in which John Philips, invited he said by his Native Soil, expands the theme of 'what Care is due to Orchats'. You feel that he is deeply, devotedly interested, and he carries you with him, grafting, pruning, discussing what soil each particular apple loves; but he is most engaging in the lively glimpses he gives of happenings in an orchard. He uses his eyes closely, affectionately; he is curious, observant, and whether he watches

> the little Race of Birds, that hop
> From Spray to Spray, scooping the costliest fruit
> Insatiate, undisturb'd,

or looks through a magnifying glass at mites—those 'wonderful artists'—he is enthralled by the processes of nature. As to pests, the more tiresome they are, the more absorbed does he become:

> Myriads of Wasps now also clustering hang,
> And drain a spurious Honey from the Groves,
> Their Winter Food; tho' oft repuls'd, again

> They rally, undismay'd; but Fraud with ease
> Ensnares the noisom Swarms; let ev'ry Bough
> Bear frequent Vials, pregnant with the Dregs
> Of *Moyle*, or *Mum*, or *Treacle's* viscous Juice;
> They, by th'alluring Odor drawn, in haste
> Fly to the dulcet Cates, and crouding sip
> Their palatable Bane; joyful thou'lt see
> The clammy Surface all o'er-strown with Tribes
> Of greedy Insects, that with fruitless Toil
> Flap filmy Pennons oft, to extricate
> Their Feet, in liquid Shackles bound.

The observation is acute, one might say sympathetic, as in Pope's little snapshot:

> Not closer, orb in orb conglobed are seen,
> The buzzing bees about their dusky queen.

Not that I am claiming that *The Dunciad* is a nature poem—only that Pope had seen bees swarming, and had noticed them, just as he had the dabchick that 'waddles in the copse, On feet and wings, and flies and wades and hops'.

We note, however, that delight was not the sole reaction to country life. Thus Diaper feelingly throws out:

> All do not love in clotting Fields to sweat,
> Where clayie Fallows clog the labouring Feet:

and he can give as wilderness a view of the country as ever Crabbe did a hundred years later. His poem *Brent* (*c.* 1712) is wet, soggy, marshy, full of the vapours of the fens. Moreover,

> No joyous birds here stretch their tunefull throats
> And pierce the yielding air with thrilling notes,
> But the hoarse seapies with an odious cry
> Skim o'er the marsh, and tell what storms are nigh. . . .

a revulsion against the conventional pretty-pretty which was carried on in Richards's *Hoglandiae Descriptio* of 1710, and in an anonymous *Lincolnshire* in 1720. These people indeed knew what the country could be like, as did Stephen Duck, who talks about it intimately in what is almost his only tolerable poem, *The Thresher's Labour* (1730), knowing, in contrast with Walsh, that constant peace does not attend the fields. He had, himself, got in the wheat. He is best, as you would expect from his sub-name 'the thresher poet', on that labour, which he did not pretend was pleasant. The shepherd might well tune his voice to sing among the fountains, the linnets, and the lambkins, but

> When sooty Pease we thresh, you scarce can know
> Our native Colour, as from Work we go;
> The Sweat, the Dust, and suffocating Smoak,
> Make us so much like *Ethiopians* look,
> We scare our Wives, when Ev'ning brings us home:
> And frighted Infants think the Bugbear come.

There was nothing in all this to please the Victorians in enlarging the soul. What was found wanting in the early part of this century was what was called 'metaphysical tension', which was hankered after perhaps exaggeratedly; today we seem to prefer the grumbling attitude, the poetry of dissatisfaction. The value of the poetry of the period under discussion resides in its honesty, its attempt to say, as Swift put it, 'something in verse as true as prose'. The poets were not to be led away by words, by the yoking together, however, gentle, of heterogeneous ideas. Granville had warned them against 'unnatural flights in poetry'. There is little plunging below the surface, for that is not *common* sense: the business of the nature poet was to voice what 'oft was seen but ne'er so plainly exprest', for the *esprit simpliste* of the period made the poets react against the indirect, the oblique. The virtue of their poetry lies, we might say, in its attempt to achieve an exact correspondence between the thing and the words, so that the corresponding emotion might be aroused: that is where the tension arises, not in the clash of ideas. Its grace—in both senses of the word—lies in its economy, and in its making good the claim that ordinary sentiments were proper material for poetry. When the poets were evocative, as they sometimes were (though they were never incantatory), it was not from vagueness, but from precision, not from enticing the reader into unchartered realms, but from wishing to fix him firmly in the realm of feelings shared. The appeal was not to adventure, to a reassessment of reality, but to intensified recognition. These poets spur you to look more closely, to listen more attentively than you did before, to go beyond careless, impercipient attention. As a mild example we can take William Broome, even in a Pastoral, that deliberately unreal, but often delightful form of restricted chamber-music, designed, in Tickell's phrase, to create a 'pleasing delusion' removed from nature. Broome (*c.* 1720) makes you observe deer even more alertly than Thomson does:

> The timid deer, swift-starting as they gaze,
> Bound off in crowds, then turn again and gaze.

On the other hand, they might be too plain, too simple, thus making undue demands on the reader's co-operation. We have, for example, Samuel Croxall in *The Vision* (1715):

> Pensive beneath a spreading oak I stood,
> That veil'd the hollow channel of the flood:
> Along whose shelving banks the violet blue
> And primrose pale in lovely mixture grew.
> High over-arch'd the bloomy woodbine hung,
> The gaudy goldfinch from the maple sung. . . .
> Here ev'ry flower that Nature's pencil draws
> In various kinds a bright enamel rose;
> The silver dazy streak'd with ruddy light,
> The yellow cowslip, and the snow-drop white;
> The fragrant hyacinth. . . .

and so on, in a cumulative catalogue of many lines.

There is nothing striking, no imagery even by way of comparison; and indeed it might be said of many a poet up to the middle 'twenties of the century, that

> A primrose by the river's brim
> A yellow primrose was to him

and he did not see why it should be anything more. Was it not enough that it should delight? They did not all realize that something had to be done with the primrose, the spreading oak, or the hollow channel of the flood, to make the object part of a pattern. Yet very little sense of pattern, provided the vision was intent enough, the words precise enough, could produce an object conveying a heightened, almost jolting appreciation of nature. Take as a clear example Ambrose Philips's *Winter Piece* (1709), of which a few lines may be quoted, known to repletion though they may be:

> And yet but lately have I seen, e'en here
> The Winter in a lovely Dress appear.
> E'er yet the Clouds let fall the treasur'd Snow,
> Or Winds begun thro' hazy Skies to blow.
> At Ev'ning a keen Eastern Breeze arose;
> And the descending Rain unsullied froze.
> Soon as the silent shades of Night withdrew,
> The ruddy Morn disclos'd at once to View
> The Face of Nature in a rich Disguise,
> And brighten'd ev'ry Object to my Eyes.
> For ev'ry Shrub, and ev'ry Blade of Grass,
> And ev'ry pointed Thorn seem'd wrought in Glass.
> In Pearls and Rubies rich the Hawthorns show,
> While thro' the Ice the Crimson Berries glow.

And later:

> When if a sudden Gust of Wind arise,
> The brittle Forrest into Atoms flies;
> The crackling Wood beneath the Tempest bends,
> And in a spangl'd Show'r the Prospect ends.

Philips is sensing it all keenly. It is deliberately a still piece, not to be aligned with, say, Cotton's boisterous *Winter* (*c.* 1680). There is not a striking word through the whole poem, no original simile, hardly a simile at all. And, if we think of it,

G

is there not a great deal to be said for liking a thing for its own sake, for seeing the object as it really is? Not to have to think in terms of somebody else's mind, or feel with somebody else's feeling? Might we not lament with George Eliot 'that intelligence so rarely shows itself in speech without metaphor—that we can so seldom declare what a thing is, except by saying it is something else?' And with Philips the picture is, though innocent of metaphor, not dead nor flat; it is a stereoscopic vision contrived by the sensitive adaptation of words to the thing delightedly seen. It is precise, accurate observation, a concise record of objects; but we respond also—as Professor Geoffrey Tillotson has pointed out—to the repetition of 'ev'ry', to the careful choice of adjectives—'brittle', 'crackling', 'spangl'd'. Mercifully there is no comment, since Philips tactfully respects his reader (except for a fanciful little snippet about Merlin at the end); and the result is a holding picture, seen through a glacial transparency. It compels us to use our imagination to be ourselves creative.

Yet we of today may still feel with the Victorians that something is lacking. This poetry does not quite get us 'there'. Is this, we ask, to use Wordsworth's phrase, 'the . . . language of man in a state of vivid sensation'? Does it give us 'that sort of pleasure, and that quantity of pleasure, [which] may be imparted, and which a Poet may rationally endeavour to impart'? What we look for, presumably, is that sense of something— and here that 'something' is nature—which compels us to give the whole of our awareness, the whole of our being, for that particular moment; so that, at that particular moment, for that moment, nothing else exists. We arrive, in fact, at an aesthetic experience. We may be made alert by the *Winter Piece*, but we are not wholly absorbed, may indeed remain wholly outside, as spectators. With Parnell possibly we get closer to this aesthetic experience, in what, again, is a well-known poem, *A Night-Piece on Death* (*c.* 1715). We can extract from great stretches of moralizing and generalizing, what strikes us as the utterance of a man in a vivid state of sensation which he can to some degree impart:

> How deep yon Azure dies the Sky!
> Where Orbs of Gold unnumber'd lye,
> While thro' their Ranks in silver pride
> The nether crescent seems to glide.
> The slumb'ring Breeze forgets to breathe,
> The Lake is smooth and clear beneath,
> Where once again the spangled Show
> Descends to meet our Eyes below.
> The Grounds which on the right aspire,
> In dimness from the View retire;
> The Left presents a Place of Graves,
> Whose wall the silent Water laves.
> That Steeple guides the doubtful Sight
> Among the livid gleams of Night.

The words are chosen with careful accuracy; the *nether* crescent; it is, and looks lower, and *seems* to glide; when we look at the reflection of the stars, they appear to descend; objects do *retire* from the view in dimness. It is the pattern of recognition that gives us the aesthetic experience. We get something of the same effect in *Windsor Forest*, not from the insistence upon details of colour in birds and fish, and in the general landscape painting, but in such lines as:

> Here waving Groves a chequer'd Scene display,
> And part admit and part exclude the Day. . . .
> There, interspers'd in Lawns and opening Glades,
> Thin trees arise that shun each others' Shades.

But we get, one may feel, the holding, almost breath-taking sense of the actuality of what we see and hear from Lady Winchilsea, notably in *A Nocturnal Reverie*. Visually, perhaps, not more than others can give us; but what is so sure, so compelling, apart from the primitive fear, is the auditory image, itself an experience, though inevitably connected with the actual experience, or it would convey little:

When the loos'd Horse now, at his Pasture leads,
Comes slowly grazing thro' th'adjoining Meads,
Whose stealing Pace, and lengthen'd Shade we fear,
Till torn up Forage in his Teeth we hear.

That is possibly as intense, as unerringly directed, as anything
in the first few years of the century; and in *The Bird* Lady
Winchilsea gives something of the same intensity by working
on the visual imagination:

Soft in thy notes and in thy dress,
Softer than numbers can express,
Softer than love, softer than light
When first escaping from the night,
When first she rises, unarray'd,
And steals a passage thro' the shade.

The personification, lightly sketched in as it is, may for some
readers interfere with the impact: but does not the passage give
as well as anywhere to be found, the actual sense of dawn in a
wood?

Naturally, during the first forty years of this century, there
were changes in interest, in stimulus. It is impossible to make a
neat schema, since mankind is distressingly ill-drilled; some
poets insist on being ahead of their time, while others lag
shockingly behind. Yet a scaffolding is convenient; and it may
serve the purpose of discussion to watch the poetry of the
period building itself up to the contemplative, philosophic
nature-poetry which is its distinction, by absorbing into the
enjoying, noticing, structure sketched in above a number of
other impulses and attitudes. First one can note the cult of
wildness, which, with so many other elements, reached its
height in the late 'twenties. It used to be the fashion to believe that the country poet of this age was concerned only with
what was useful, comfortable, even utilitarian: that it is typified
by Thomson's preference (in one, rather rare mood) for

> softly smiling Hills,
> On which the Power of Cultivation lies,

and that the people of those days regarded anything more than a gentle slope as a 'horrid Alp'. Yet even Thomas Burnet, who in his *Theory of the Earth* (1681) argued that mountains were a sad mistake, admitted that 'these majestic ruins cast the Mind into a pleasing kind of Stupor and Admiration': Dennis looked at the Alps with 'a delightful horrour and terrible joy'; for Shaftesbury, who shared these emotions, this was to be 'deep in the romantick way'. And even if many agreed with Defoe that mountain ranges merely formed convenient trade boundaries, Philips, in *Cyder*, ventured to say:

> Nor are the Hills unamiable, whose Tops
> To Heav'n aspire, affording Prospect sweet,
> To Human Ken;

while Blackmore in *Creation* (1712), far bolder, declared that:

> The mountains more sublime in aether rise,
> Transfix the clouds, and tow'r amidst the skies;
> The snowy fleeces, which their heads involve
> Still stay in part, and still in part dissolve;
> Torrents, and loud impetuous cataracts
> Through roads abrupt, and rude unfashion'd tracts
> Roll down the lofty mountain's channel'd sides,
> And unto the vale convey their foaming tides—

a feeling ecstatically echoed by Horace Walpole when, as a young man, he wrote to West about crossing the Alps. And long before, Berkeley's Philonous had asked Hylas:

> At the prospect of the wide and deep ocean, or some huge mountain whose top is lost in the clouds, or of an old gloomy forest, are not our minds filled with a pleasing horror? Even in rocks and deserts, is there not an agreeable wildness?

Although Aaron Hill might write in some scorn of 'that blood-curdling chilling Influence of Nature, working on our Passions

(which Cricks call the Sublime)', that did not prevent Mallet
getting satisfaction from the idea of the Caucasian mountains

> Pale glitt'ring with eternal Snows to Heav'n,

or Moses Browne experiencing a thrill from the 'shudd'ring
Horror' that precipices and mountains, frowned, as he put it,
on his aching sight.

All this was very much aided by the new vogue for landscape painting, which affected the poets, including Thomson,
who became like other men enamoured of

> What'er Lorrain light-touched with softening hue,
> Or savage Rosa dashed, or learned Poussin drew.

Grongar Hill (1726) is in the main such a landscape. A poet, such
as Dyer, who began life as a painter, would dwell upon the
scene broadening as he winds about the chequered side of the
hill, until

> Below me trees unnumbered rise
> Beautiful in various dyes. . . .
> Gaudy as the opening dawn,
> Lies a long and level lawn,
> On which a dark hill, steep and high,
> Holds and charms the wandering eye!
> Deep are his feet in Towy's flood,
> His sides are clothed with waving wood,
> And ancient towers crown his brow,
> That cast an awful look below.

It is clear that the interest in the country, in nature, has shifted.
What produces poetry now is not the fascination of detail for
itself, but of detail only in so far as it gives perspective to a
wider landscape. This is emphatically so with Thomson; his
set pieces, his thunderstorm, and especially his snowstorm,
are triumphantly convincing. Yet we might adapt to him the
remark Professor Elton made about Swinburne: 'The *Forsaken
Garden* and *Winter in Northumberland*, though never definite in

drawing, give the very atmosphere of the place and weather.' In Thomson's *Winter* (1726), the snowflakes, for all the detail about them, are never intimately pictured: they are

> At first, thin-wavering; till at last, the Flakes
> Fall broad, and wide, and fast, dimming the Day,
> With a continual Flow . . .

the result being excitingly (in the second printing) 'one wild dazzling Waste'. He can be particular, as with the all too be-Christmas-carded robin, but he prefers not to be.

And together with his expansion of vision there came into the nature poetry of this time an interest at the opposite end of the scale, an immense curiosity about the lower end of the Great Chain of Being. Not only in wasps or mites, with John Philips, or in spiders, with Pope in that penetratingly emphatic couplet.

> The spider's touch, how exquisitely fine!
> Feels at each thread, and lives along the line:

but in microbes. We meet this in William Diaper's *Dryades* (1712). True, he is fascinated by fireflies, is curiously interested in the working of ants, and his eye is always on the object. *Dryades*, incidentally, apart from being mildly pleasurable in itself, is an oddly foreshadowing poem; for, before Thomson, Diaper was vocal about the progression of the seasons and the effects of changing light. In comparison with *Dryades*, *Windsor Forest* is a static landscape: it is a 'place' rather than a 'nature' poem. But the point of interest here is the curiosity Diaper exhibits in what the microscope reveals, and the suggested implications:

> Men Nature in her secret Work behold,
> Untwist her Fibres, and her Coats unfold
> With Pleasure trace the Threads of stringy Roots,
> The various Textures of the ripening Fruits;

> And animals, who careless live at ease,
> To whom the Leaves are Worlds, the Drops are Seas.
> If to the finish'd Whole so little goes,
> How small the Parts that must the Whole compose. . . .
> The azure Dye, which Plums in Autumn boast,
> That handled fades, and at a Touch is lost,
> (Of fairest Show) is all a living Heap;
> And round their little World the lovely Monsters creep. . . .

a theme Henry Brooke was to take up some twenty years later when in *Universal Beauty* (1735) he wrote:

> Of Azure Tribes that in the Damson bloom,
> And paint the Regions of the rip'ning Plum.

But this kind of observation was soon absorbed in the realm of scientific rather than of nature poetry, much of the former to be classed with those didactic poems which, in Saintsbury's phrase, 'so fearfully overcast or overbilge the poetry of the time'. One wonders if he has descended to the depths with Henry Baker's *The Universe* or plunged to the bottomless pit with Richard Collin's *Nature Display'd*, or even trifled with Desaguilers.

But then, as the author of a moralistic poem, *An Essay on Human Life* (2nd ed. 1736), wrote in his Preface:

> Of all Kinds of Poetry the *Didascalic* is the most valuable . . . the Descriptive Kind is like a fine Landskip, where you meet with two or three principal Figures; the rest is all Rocks, Rivulets, hanging Woods and verdant Lawns, amusing to the Eye, shewing the Taste of the Painter, but carrying little Instruction along with it . . .

Even in the earlier years of the century writers seem to have felt that just to look at nature was not enough, and would have agreed with Pope when he said to Warton that 'a poem consisting wholly of description would be like a meal made up of sauces'. From the first the moralistic would keep breaking in. The passage just quoted from Diaper ends:

> Who would on Colour dote, or pleasing Forms,
> If Beauty, when discover'd, is but Worms?

and John Philips tells us the doom of his wasps is what 'Waits Luxury, and lawless Love of Gain'. The tendency was pervasive, and is best known in Dyer's

> A little Rule, a little Sway,
> A Sunbeam on a Winter's Day,
> Is all the proud and mighty have,
> Between the Cradle and the Grave.

Morality, however, soon expanded into an ethical vision, which acted as the loom which wove together the threads here indicated. 'Nature' had either to be a framework for, or a *décor* behind, human beings; or, spelt with a very capital N, substance for philosophic meditation, based largely upon the science of the day. The area dealing with the spectrum has been beautifully dealt with by Professor Marjorie Nicolson in her brilliant and entertaining *Newton Demands the Muse*, and will be avoided here so far as possible. Yet it is worth noticing that descriptions of the solar or galactic systems as treated by Blackmore in *The Creation*, and Mallet in Canto II of *The Excursion* (1728)—an exhilarating piece of work—produced images which do not compare badly with Shelley's in *Queen Mab*, and are in a sense 'nature' poetry. And in becoming scientific, nature poetry became the vehicle of the reverent Deism which came to pervade the age.

For the wedding of nature with the scientific discoveries of the time gave rise to a feeling of awe that voluntary moved harmonious numbers. The phrase 'renascence of wonder', usually applied to the 'romantic' age is just as applicable here, though the fount of wonder was different. For the Augustans it arose from an awareness of the marvels of nature, for the Romantics at seeing themselves as part of nature, though this sense was not altogether lacking in the Augustans. The wonder was born largely from the realization of how marvellously everything was fitted, not so much to the individual mind, but within itself. For it the age had passed from a theocentric conception to, for good or ill, an anthropocentric one, it had not proceeded, for better or worse, to the egocentric one, which the Victorians, descendants of Wordsworth, expected to find implicit in their poetry. So it was knowing how things worked in nature that produced poetic pressure; as Akenside declared in 1744:

>   Nor ever yet
> The melting rainbow's vernal-tinctured hues
> To me have shown so pleasing, as when first
> The hand of science pointed out the path
> In which the sunbeams, gleaming from the West
> Fall on a wat'ry cloud.

The emotions nature poetry worked upon were such as might be derived from grasping, to use the title of Ray's book, 'the Wisdom of God manifested in the Works of the Creation'. Nature poems became a *Benedicite*.

One may take in illustration another very well-known passage, one from Thomson's *To the Memory of Sir Isaac Newton*.

>   Did ever poet image aught so fair
> Dreaming in whisp'ring groves by the hoarse brook?
> Or prophet, to whose rapture Heav'n descends?
> Even now the setting sun and shifting clouds,
> Seen, Greenwich, from thy lovely heights, declare,
> How just, how beauteous, the refractive law.

It is hardly Thomson's fault that the occasion of this paean does not appeal to us as it did to him. It may seem bathos. The sunset was lovely, as Thomson appreciated as well as anybody: but to him what was really marvellous was the way it came about. That was the stupendous thing. For Thomson and his generation philosophy did not clip an angel's wings; on the contrary, it was precisely what made them grow. They would simply not have understood the attitude of the Romantics; they might, alas! have regarded it as immature, and have quoted, 'All knowledge begins and ends as wonder; but the wonder that is the child of ignorance must be replaced by the wonder that is the parent of adoration.' The poetry of the 1720's was witness to the renascence of the second kind of wonder; that of most of the Romantics might have seemed to them like the gaping of bucolics. Yet wonder was not enough. The thinking, feeling man could go beyond this to a conception of the moral governance of the universe. Happy the man who knows the causes of things; the Virgilian tag echoes through much of *The Seasons*. To such a man, endowed with an 'exalting eye',

> A fairer World
> Of which the Vulgar never had a Glimpse
> Displays its Charms; whose Minds are richly fraught
> With Philosophic Stores, superior Light. . . .

It would seem indeed, that Thomson found after the first flush of youthful reaction, that merely to reflect his sense-impressions of the country was not enough to release his imagination, and so enlarge that of his readers. This he did, apart from deepening his theme with near-religious cogitations, by vividly apprehending what a wide reading had offered him, and *creating* the visual image. He becomes, it is true, a little tedious when he tells us how nice it is to sit down in the shade on a hot day:

> Welcome, ye Shades! ye bow'ry Thickets, hail!

and so on, for a dozen or so lines. He awakens little in us, though he may have evoked happy recognition in contemporary readers. But he achieves an altogether different, and magnificent, awakening impact on the imagination when he writes of:

> where the Northern Ocean, in vast whirls
> Boils round the naked, melancholy isles
> Of farthest Thule, and th' Atlantic surge
> Pours in among the stormy Hebrides,

> Who can recount what transmigrations there
> Are annual made, what nations come and go?
> And how the living clouds on clouds arise,
> Infinite wings! till all the plume-dark air
> And rude resounding shores are one wild cry?

The further he travels from his own experience the more vivid
he becomes. In Russia he met (in imagination) the bear
'shaggy with ice', and the 'furry Russian' in his sled, who

> by his reindeer drawn, behind him throws
> A shining Kingdom in a Winter's Day.

And when he goes as far back as the Deluge with 'fabling
Burnet', he can splendidly describe how the waters 'rush im-
petuous',

> Till, from the Centre to the streaming Clouds
> A shoreless Ocean tumbled round the Globe.

The last image may come from 'Sea cover'd Sea, Sea without
Shore' in *Paradise Lost*, but the phasing is his, and the evocative word 'tumbled'.

And how rare, we may think, the vivifying word in most
of the nature poetry of the period, as though in taking their
readers' sensibility for granted the poets too readily employed
the word to hand. And how our perceptions are quickened
when we hap upon some unusual word, or an extremely apt
usage! When, for instance, John Philips tells us that 'Now the
Fowler . . . with swift early steps, Treads the *crimp* earth'; or
Diaper remarks that 'Worms o'er moistened Clods their
folding bodies trail'; or when Savage, in that very derivative
poem *The Wanderer*, says that the stars as they 'Cross ether swift
elance the vivid fires', or bids us note how 'berries blacken on
the *virid* thorn'. So too Mallet, in the rather dull first Canto of
The Excursion rouses us from too placid acceptance by noting
that when the earthquake is impending, 'a sighing cold
Winters the shadow'd air'; or in one of those passages,

consisting of what can be described as 'romantic trappings' so common in the period from Garth's *Claremont* (1715) onwards, he says:

> All is dead silence here, and undisturb'd,
> Save what the wind sighs, and the wailing owl
> Screams *solitary* to the mournful moon.

These startle, or at least awaken, because the poets did not take to heart, or were unable much to implement, Addison's dictum that 'Words, when well chosen, have so great a force in them, that a description often gives us more lively ideas [*sc.* sense of actuality] than the sight of things themselves.' What we most feel the lack of, perhaps, is the awareness of what might be called releasing, seminal imagery. They use images, as Mr. Day Lewis has noted, 'to make a point or outline a picture, rather than to rocket the poem into a stratosphere of infinite meaning'. Moreover, as often as not in that period, the symbols for the emotions are themselves the things that caused the emotions: thus figurative imagery would have been largely out of place. 'There is a poetry', Goethe said, 'without figures of speech which is a single figure of speech.' It is to this category that much poetry of this time belongs. It is we who fail in imagination if we do not react.

For if the nature poetry of the early eighteenth century differs from that of our own day, it need not for that seem removed. True, it runs in none of the ruts indicated by the changing fashions of our own era: it lacks irony, it is empty of the delights of ambiguity, it does not seek to reconcile opposites. The imagination of the poets, fed by what the eye applied to the mind, was contemplative rather than dialectical. If we accept its idiom, go to it simply for what it can give—an intense appreciation of the delights that nature offers—it can impart lively pleasure and so acquire positive value: while to those of us who are enriched, or even only entertained, by understanding how a generation felt, and strove to share what it felt, this poetry can bring refreshment, and something of the 'peace of the Augustans' which they themselves, after all, achieved at a time of crises not incomparable with our own. We may feel humble before so worthwhile an achievement. It is not without its meaning.

CRÉBILLON FILS

*The Sofa: A Moral Tale**

O UR own generation of English readers is perhaps suffering from the fact that there is an extraordinary gap in our literature that does not exist in the French. It is possible that, if we had a series of works dealing more or less subtly with love in all its forms, we might have been saved the torment of pretentious sex-novels, whose appeal is entirely luscious and unintellectual (and therefore sentimental) with which this century has been deluged. In English literature there is none— or practically none—of that pondered, delicate and indelicate but always polished, treatment of love of which eighteenth-century French literature is full, none of those vivid memoirs which are so entertaining to historian, psychologist, and novel-reader alike. Our nearest approach is, probably, Sterne's *Sentimental Journey* on the one hand, and Smollett's *Peregrine Pickle*, with its *Memoirs of a Lady of Quality* on the other. As a result we have no *Adolphe*, no *Chartreuse de Parme*, for such masterpieces can come only as the result of a long tradition, including such works as *Les Liaisons Dangereuses*, itself a fine achievement, a tradition to which philosophers of the rank of Diderot were proud to add. Perhaps a perusal of their works, even in translation, may, by setting an example in form, improve our taste in these matters: for who among the writers of this century, except George Moore, has given us a

---

* Introduction to Crébillon Fils, *The Sofa: A Moral Tale*, Routledge and Kegan Paul, 1927; republished by the Folio Society, 1952.

glimpse of what such things may be?[1] For in this respect our literary tradition has been unfortunate. Our Elizabethan song-writers stated the problems of love, but none elucidated them, though Donne was on the edge of analysis. The triumph of Puritanism, momentarily broken during the Restoration period, which did not, however, have the leisure essential to the subject, held such enquiries at a prohibitive distance; while the Romantic movement, denying the physical basis of love (with the possible exception of Byron), passing through puerility, has rotted to neurasthenia and prurience. Translation cannot fill our gap, but it may induce us to do so, for we should rescue psychology from between the covers of textbooks, and, basing it upon experience and sensibility, use it as material for works of art.

Sensibility! that is, of course, the crux of the matter; and for this there must be openness and honesty, not the shamefaced lascivious peening which the libraries sometimes advertise by exclusion. Where there is no frankness there can be no art. For however much the French 'little classics' may shock the prude or make the coward tremble, they are by no means fitted to be guide-books for callow Don Juans. Always and every-where these authors, Bibiéna, de la Morlière, de Boufflers, and Crébillon himself, insist upon the essential ingredients of sensibility and delicacy in love, upon a profound and sensitive understanding of the complex human being. What other safe-guard is there against the bitter disillusion of the flesh-weary rake? Again and again they point out that if you seek to gratify the senses alone you will reap only tares, for the senses can never be satisfied for long. It would be overshooting the mark to say that the works of these *conteurs* are stern lessons in morality; they are not. They are, however, graceful inductions into something far harder to compass than rigid morality; they aim at the perilous balance of sympathy and understanding

---

[1] Though this was written in 1927, no work, even the Alexandrian series of Mr. Lawrence Durrell, has led me to change my opinion. B.D. 1968.

accompanying physical pleasure for, while they deal largely with the body, they never forget the soul. This is true of the long list that includes, not only those already mentioned, but the Abbé Prévost, from whom Richardson might seem to derive: Meusnier de Querlon, Benseval, in a sense Chateaubriand, and in our own day Raymond Radiguet and M. Julien Benda, not to mention Marcel Proust. They vary throughout the centuries as the tradition develops and manners alter but those of the eighteenth century present a remarkably homogeneous body.

De Boufflers, it is true, is something different from the normal *conteur* of his day, for apart from the fact that he dealt more directly than most with the social life of his time, he achieved a natural completeness of form which leaves one perfectly satisfied. And there is, besides, an unusual humane element in his work, born of contact with many different classes, races and creeds, for he was at one time Governor of Senegal, where he seems to have been universally liked. Yet, in spite of his contact with the world, he had some of that naïf simpleness that we associate with Rousseau, and he believed in the simple affections. There is a tenderness in his gaiety foreign to the work of Crébillon fils, and one might even say that he was ever so little a sentimentalist, not enough to distort life, but enough to add a ribbon to its costume. Not that it is fair to say that Crébillon was altogether unromantic, but his is the romance of social relations, as in the story of Zulema and Phenima (in *The Sofa*), and one must confess that for him romance was apt to be in Chamfort's famous phrase, *le contact de deux épidermes*.

For Crébillon liked things to be clear-cut, and this is what makes him the accurate and cool observer that he is. That alone should serve to clear him from the charge of being a purveyor of aphrodisiac writings, even if his intent were not throughout satirical. Yet the issue must not be confused: he was not satirical in the cause of prig-righteousness, but in that

H

of refinement and frankness. In any case, the morality of his time as regards sex was not that commonly recognized by the Churches in England: it was rather that of the Courts of Love of troubadour France, where not the choice of a lover was important, but the manner of loving. Yet again, it is never the merely physical that counts; there must be grace and delicacy, a degree of understanding, and above all the game of love must, like every other game, be played according to certain rules.

That particular portion of eighteenth-century society in which Crébillon moved definitely tried to make love a part of the social texture, for whatever love might be—and Crébillon was far too wise to think that he had discovered this secret— love-making was a rational social pleasure. It was the great time-killer, and, as happens frequently through the ages, it was a superb subject for conversation. For wherever there is leisure, love, of the kind worth talking about, thrives, and each age creates its own special kind. That which belongs to this period is probably best ranked under the heading Stendhal described as *amour goût*, though it was soon to be replaced by the *amour passion* of such as Julie de Lespinasse and Benjamin Constant. Thus for Crébillon, wherever *goût*, friendship, mutual inclination and respect are lacking, there can be no love, only lust, and his aversion from this is best shown in his story of Amina. But for this love to be happy, it must be frank, free from sophistry, and not arrived at by intricate false thinking, as it was with Mochles and Almahide. Nor must there be any false prudery, as exhibited in the cruel story of Zuleika, nor coxcomb pretensions as with Mazulim. But however much coarse lovers are to be reprehended, Crébillon never saw the need for indignation, and thus he coolly laid their vices bare with no more scorn than is needed to give a certain salt to his story. In spite of the airy, unmoral gaiety of his manner, we are never allowed to forget the satiric intent, although to some it may appear that the pill is too thickly covered with gilding to make it at all effective. Yet, to his own time, he did not appear to err on this side, as his letters to Chesterfield indicate, and amazing and unusual as his stories may appear to be, he will scarcely be accused of exaggerating by any who have read the memoirs of, say, the Ducs de Richelieu or Lauzun, or of Benseval, or the Comte de Tilly. Indeed, to many people of his time he was felt to be too near the truth, and some of them took their revenge.

Not only *Le Sopha* but his earliest tales are placed in an Oriental milieu, not to make them fantastic but to give him greater freedom to deal personal strokes and bring his satire home. In this way he was only following the example of Montesquieu, but it did not save him from prison. He was, perhaps, a little too determined to show that by Agra he meant Paris. His bored Shah—and was ever monarch more bored than Louis XV?—dwells in a realm where patchwork and embroidery are the rage, as they were, according to Marmontel, in Paris. Nor need we go to French sources to realize this, for the Earl Marshal writing to Hume during his stay in Paris, says: 'I hope we shall not get back a dandy, a dapper man at the embroidering'. And this is only one of a hundred touches to bring the matter close, and to suggest that it was no distant society he was speaking of; and, seeing that he was a Parisian of Parisians it was hardly to be expected of him.

He was born on the 12th of February, 1707, only a fortnight after his parents were married. His father, Prosper Jolyot de Crébillon, who appears to us as a rather grim lawyer and writer of grimmer tragedies of blood nobody is now ashamed of leaving unread, was at that time sunning himself in the success of his *Atrée et Thyeste*, which was frequently performed at Court. The boy, Claude Prosper, after a period at a Jesuit school, thus grew up in those unequivocally gay Regency days which gave him so much of his material, and began his literary life by collaborating with the Italian actors in some light satirical pieces for their theatre, which were not modelled upon his father's, for those he could never find time to read.

The old lawyer had by now fallen upon evil days; he had secured no Court pickings, except some minor treasury post which had expired in 1721: his father had died insolvent, and his wife (at any rate penniless) was dead. He retired to a garret, which he shared with dogs, cats and ravens, and, like a true sage neglected food and cleanliness—but not tobacco—until, in 1731, he became one of the immortal forty. The wisdom of his son was of a different order, and flitting about as a gay and lettered man of the Town, frequenting *sociétés joyeuses* with Cayliss and others, he gained the patronage of the dowager Princesse de Conti.

He was soon to need it, for in 1734 he published *L'Écumoire, ou Tanzaï et Néadarné, histoire japonaise*, a scarcely disguised satire which caused a terrific uproar among the rulers and the elect. He was aiming at the Papal Bull *Unigenitus;* he was undermining the Monarchy itself; worse, he was lampooning the Cardinal de Rohan, the High Priest Sogrenutio was undoubtedly the Bishop of Rennes, and the fairy Cucumber was too obviously the Duchesse du Maine. The book was at once suspended 'on account of its indecencies and certain portraits which were easily interpreted'. Anything might happen to a rash young man from the fury of outraged dignitaries, and, to save his skin, Cardinal Fleury had him placed in the Bastille, or so it is always said, though he was actually admitted to the prison of Vincennes on December the 8th, 1734. The rhymesters of the time, delighted to have a fresh subject for their rapid pens, sang:

> Pour un conte de Cendrillon
> Agence de quelque boutille,
> Notre pauvre ami Crébillon
> Vient d'être mis à la Bastille;
> Depuis qu'il est au galbanon
> Il s'en faut beaucoup qu'il babille,
> Car il est sérieux ce dit-on,
> Comme un âne que l'on étrille.

But he was not there for long. The Princesse de Conti had him released, heaping coals of fire on his head with a 'reproof which could not have been more gracious or tender-hearted'. In his book he had described his heroine to be 'absent-minded as a princess', and Madame de Conti on releasing him said: 'You see, all princesses are not absent-minded.' Her favour, however, did not save him from five years' exile from Paris, which he spent largely at Sens.

But all times remain in some ways much the same, and the interdiction of his book made it only the more sought after, to the greater profit of the booksellers. The ladies especially were eager to get it, and though pious abbés and severe lords lieutenants in the provinces deplored it, lost no opportunity of reading it. It made them very sorry for Crébillon *père*, especially as some thought that he was the author, and not all Claude's protestations that it had been printed at the printing-house of the *Nouvelles Ecclésiastiques* could make them accept as good literature what they admitted to be a true picture of manners. 'Paris is mad, and this work has been over-estimated; good taste is dead; to succeed nowadays a man must write imbecilities.' No matter, such garbage would soon rot into oblivion; it would be like that ridiculous book translated from the English, *Gulliver's Travels;* it would be the rage for a few days, and then would sink into well-deserved obscurity. Voltaire also thought that Paris was mad, not for liking the book which had brightened his solitude, but for putting Crébillon in prison.

When the young man returned to Paris he found his father, not only Censor Royal, but once more a famous play-wright, so successful as to arouse the competitive spirit in Voltaire, who rehandled no fewer than five of his plays. But father and son were not on good terms. When asked in conversation which of his works he thought the best, the old man replied that he did not know: but, he added, pointing to his son, 'That one is undoubtedly my worst.' Claude retorted,

referring to a report that Prosper was not the author of his plays
by giving as a reason that the son could not but be his father's
own handiwork, and that whatever might be said of the plays,
Crébillon *fils* was not *des Chartreux*. For the latter moved in a
different circle, and wherever he went gained a reputation for
kindliness, honesty, and general good behaviour, in spite of a
certain tendency to gibe at his father, much to the astonishment of the nineteenth-century commentators, who seem to have
been unable to reconcile decent living with clear-headedness
as to love. Jocund his muse was, and though it would be rash
to say that his life was chaste, it was never scandalous. Yet
it had some excuse for being so, and one of his adventures
gives us a clue as to his attitude of hatred towards inconstant
women. Just before the publication of his first book he fell in
love with an actress called Gaussin, who promised to marry
him. The elated lover posted off gaily to Fontainebleau to have
the marriage-contract drawn, but coming back to Paris with it
in his pocket, was told that his speed had been wasted, or had
not been great enough. For in the interval his actress had found a
rich Milanese, and remarked coldly, but with obvious common
sense, that having got a lover she no longer needed a husband.

It is possible that this lady was immortalized in *Le Sopha*,
which appeared in 1740, in contravention, we may note, of a
Royal Decree which had forbidden its publication. This again,
of course, helped only to advertise it the more: it sold
widely, and the author was exiled to a distance of fifty leagues
from Paris. But not much more than three months later he was
back to enjoy his success, which was more than satisfactory. In
the next year the book was translated into English, and was
read by Sterne, who admitted to having studied Rabelais and
Crébillon *fils* before beginning to write. Gray could exclaim,
'Be mine to read eternal new romances of Marivaux and
Crébillon.' Further, the delicacy of the author's mind so struck
Lady Henrietta Maria Stafford that she came over to France to
become his mistress in 1744, the mother of his child in 1746,

and his wife in 1748. Although, apparently a dévote, ugly, clumsy-mannered, and cross-eyed, she seems to have made Crébillon happy, and he made her a model husband.

Nevertheless, his literary success and his exemplary behaviour do not seem to have endeared him to his father, who finding that he could not both write plays such as *Catilina* and adequately carry out his censorial duties, complained that the latter were too heavy, and demanded a coadjutor. But, to Claude's surprise and indignation, the father did not suggest that this functionary should be his son. He proposed for the place an abbé called Rousseau, an academic laureate. This attitude seemed unnatural to the son, a menace to paternal tradition; so he demanded the post, which he was prepared to take without the miserable stipend of six hundred francs that the abbé was to get. Of course, he conceded, he did not write so well as the abbé, but did the police mind about that? Yet he did not get the post, and, instead, founded the famous literary circle with Piron and Collé, which met regularly to dine at the *Caveau*.

Lady Henrietta died in about 1756, their son having died in infancy, and Claude's life began to pass into its final phase, during which he was to outlive his literary reputation. In 1759, however, he was made Censor Royal (on the retirement of his father, who lived until 1762), and was to be found at the Wednesday dinners of the Pelletier, where he may have met Garrick, Sterne and Wilkes. Certainly he corresponded with Lord Chesterfield, who doubtless saw in him something of that sound balance he would have wished to find in his son. In 1774 he became Police Censor as well, and, adding a pension to his other emoluments—some state, erroneously, that this was through the patronage of Madame de Pompadour, who had obtained him the Royal Censorship—came to the end of his life on April the 12th, 1777, in the warm aura which surrounds a comfortably situated man, a genial fellow, and a conscientious civil servant.

His works have their place in the French tradition, a little to one side of, and a little below, those of Marivaux, according to Sainte-Beuve; to Marivaux at all events he appeared worthy of attention, and recognizing himself in one of the characters of *L'Écumoire*, replied in *Le Paysan Parvenu*. 'Crébillon', he says, 'relied too much on the licentiousness of his subjects and the freedom of his tone, to attract readers; he tried to make the reader his accomplice.' To which the old officer answers: 'It is true the reader is also a man; but he is then a man at leisure, a man of taste and delicacy who expects his mind to be amused, and who is perfectly ready to be debauched, so long as it is elegantly, with politeness and decency.' To be sure, if Crébillon had wished merely to debauch the reader he might have flattered his vanity more, but that would have been to kill the satire. And if, as we may very well feel entitled to do, we regard Shah Baham in *Le Sopha* as representing the average idle reader, who calls a story that is not sportive no story at all, he could hardly have written otherwise. On the other hand there is the charming Sultana, perhaps Madame de Pompadour, who makes such admirable literary criticism, expressing, of course, Crébillon's own views. For Crébillon was an artist; otherwise his work would not have survived. The smoothness of his prose, woven together with an extraordinarily small vocabulary, is amazing. He never raises his voice, nor gesticulates so that the tale is never made to suggest deeper emotions than it can bear. If his treatment of love in *Le Sopha* is restricted to certain kinds, the limitation is deliberate, as the last remarks of the narrator prove, and in accordance with what he knew could do. It is absurd to say that he is not serious because the life of the people whom he satirized was frivolous and inane. By his very reservations he gives, as Mr. Aldous Huxley has said, 'a sort of consistency' to his creatures and their idiotic existence. And that is no mean achievement.

His literary reputation, however, has not had an altogether unchequered career. Fashionable for a time in his own day, his

books soon dropped out of popular esteem in the flood of not
very dissimilar works, though Voltaire, as we have seen,
praised him, and the Prince de Ligne thought his books worth
annotating. In the nineteenth century the growls of French
commentators grew loud against him, and the less they read
him, the more violent they became. He depicted the manners
of his time in colours that were too lively, they declared; and
so, from being the Petronius of France, he sank to the level of
'a precursor of the Marquis de Sade', a sin now venial and even
flattering, but once considered mortal. However, towards the
end of the century he was rescued by the editor of a new
edition of his work, who surely put the matter on a sound
foot when he said:

> Au xviii ième Siècle, on s'embarrassait moins de ces distinctions
> [morales] que de nos jours. La nature avait repris le dessus sur
> la convention, et les moeurs très libres acceptaient que l'on dît
> sans ambages ce que l'on faisait, ce qui se fait encore chez nous,
> mais que l'hypocrisie nous fait taire;

for though times and manners change, the human creature does
not.

BYRON'S DRAMAS*

THE place we are to give in our hearts or our esteem to Byron's dramas has always been a matter of differing opinion. In his own day, such orthodox critics as Jeffrey and Bishop Heber, while according them certain great qualities, judge them, we might think, on grounds that are often solid enough, but equally often irrelevant: on the other hand, Lockhart and Wilson give them such unstinted praise, as we in our turn may feel to be too uncritical. Bulwer Lytton regarded them as the best things that Byron ever wrote,[1] and in our own day Professor Wilson Knight, in his brilliant essay in *The Burning Oracle*, has embraced them wholeheartedly. For the most part, however, commentators have judged them harshly, even finding them 'unreadable', though now and again we hear a wilderness-crying voice pleading that they should have a place in our national repertory. What I on my part would wish to do on this occasion is to try to fit them into a Byronic pattern, and also, as far as may be, to appraise them as actable drama, aware of what would normally militate against them as such. I will say at the outset that in a sense I am inclined to agree with Lytton, for it seems to me that in some of his plays Byron is expressing more poignantly than anywhere else what he most deeply feels: and I suggest that he chose the drama as being the most concentrated form available to his self-searching genius. Perhaps the doing freed him for the writing of *Don Juan*.

* The thirty-fourth Byron Foundation Lecture delivered at the University of Nottingham, 2 March, 1962.
[1] *England and the English*, 1883.

I feel it necessary in the first place to note at what period of his life they were written, for this is of primary significance. *Manfred*, begun in Switzerland in the summer of 1816, when Byron had left England for good soon after the disastrous collapse of his marriage, was finished in the spring of the next year, when he had moved to Venice. It was not until four years later that he embarked upon the actual writing of *Marino Faliero*. In the meantime he had published—among other things, such as *Mazeppa*—the third and fourth Cantos of *Childe Harold's Pilgrimage*, markedly different in tone from the first two; *Beppo*, and the first two Cantos of the work he could refer to, with characteristic assumed carelessness, as *Donny Johnny*. Emergence from the pit? Yet when in the autumn of 1818 Shelley paid him a visit in Venice, the younger poet felt impelled to write *Julian and Maddalo*, to wit, Shelley and Byron. In his Preface he describes Maddalo as consumed by concentrated and impatient feelings, trampling on his own hopes and affections. What in that fine and terrible poem Shelley tells us about Byron may well be read as an illuminating gloss on the most striking of Byron's plays. It is clear that during the period he was brooding over and writing them, Byron was prey to the most intense emotions of pride, regret, and remorse. More than one of his characters might utter from Part III of *Childe Harold:*

> There is a very life in our despair,
> Vitality of poison—a quick root
> That feeds these deadly branches; for it were
> As nothing that we die; but Life will suit
> Itself to sorrow's most detested fruit,
> Like to the apples on the Dead Sea's shore
> All ashes to the taste.
>
> (St. xxxiv)

Luckily there was a vitality other than poison, a rapturous response to the beauty of multifarious existence that nourished the branches of Byron's abundantly creative tree.

As we all know, Byron was emphatic in stating that his dramas were designed without the remotest notion of production, his 'intercourse' with Drury Lane—as one of the Committee of Management—having given him, he declared, 'the greatest contempt' for the theatre. *Manfred*, he insisted, he composed 'actually with a *horror* of the stage, and with a view to render the thought of it impracticable' (it was, however, acted at Covent Garden in 1834), and he was furiously annoyed when *Marino Faliero*—clumsily adapted—was put on at Drury Lane in April, 1821, soon after its publication. Nevertheless they offer tempting possibilities as stage plays, and some are occasionally embodied; for instance *The Two Foscari* at the Maddermarket Theatre, Norwich; *Marino Faliero* by a society in London a few years ago; and *Cain* in Edinburgh. *Werner* at one time enjoyed considerable popularity with Macready as Werner, while *Sardanapalus* had a vogue in Germany enthusiastically supported by Kaiser Wilhelm II. If a wish to consider them as viable drama may seem impertinent to the memory of Lord Byron, one may plead in excuse a profound admiration for his far-ranging genius.

Byron's plays, we have to recognize from the outset, are philosophic statements, they are *about* something, some dominating idea, though they are divisible into two groups, which I might call the 'supernatural' and the 'human'. This is apparent from what he entitled them. *Manfred* he called 'a dramatic poem'; *Cain* and *Heaven and Earth* he classified as 'mysteries', using the mediaeval name for plays dealing with Biblical events. *The Deformed Transformed*, to be sure, though the Devil plays an active part in it, he dubbed simply 'a drama'. But this play has less profoundly philosophic thought in it than have the others, also less poetry, and one may, with Shelley, like it the least of all the things that Byron had written. It was never finished. The other plays, called 'tragedies', are peopled wholly by human beings. Although it is with these that I shall chiefly be concerned (I can deal with only one of them at all fully), the others cannot be ignored, since they would seem to state in direct terms ideas that in the 'human' plays remain as implications.

I shall begin then with *Manfred*. This, though 'supernatural' seems to have inspired, in varying degrees, the 'human' plays. Byron called it 'a kind of Poem in dialogue (in blank verse) or Drama . . . but of a very wild, metaphysical, and inexplicable kind' (To Murray, 15 February, 1817). Manfred himself is the personification of metaphysical questing rather than a person. 'tormented by a species of remorse', he is obsessed by his craving for knowledge of ultimate things—the meaning of life, of death, for a solution also of the problem of evil, crying out, as others in later plays will echo:

> Must crimes be punish'd but by other crimes,
> And greater criminals?
>
> (III. iv.)

And through various mouths in nearly all the plays we find, though modified as to the conclusion, Manfred's utterance:

> We are the fools of time and terror; Days
> Steal on us and steal from us; yet we live,
> Loathing our life, and dreading still to die.
>
> (II. ii.)

He himself longs to die, but, mysteriously,

> There is a power upon me which withholds
> And makes it my fatality to live;
>
> (I. ii.)

a theme illustrated by the Chamois Hunter clutching him as he is about to throw himself off a cliff. And again, in expressing his dilemma to Astarte:

> . . . hitherto all hateful things conspire
> To bind me in existence, in a life
> Which makes me shrink from immortality—
> A future like the past.
>
> (II. iv.)

Longing for forgetfulness, he appeals to the Spirits:

> Oblivion, self-oblivion—
> Can ye not wring from out the hidden realms
> Ye offer so profusely what I ask?
>
> (I. i.)

But 'What is death? Is there immortality?' were questions always haunting Byron. In his Detached Thoughts of 27 November, 1813, he had written:

> I see no such horror in a 'dreamless sleep', and I have no conception of any existence which duration would not render tiresome.

At this later stage, the word 'tiresome' would seem a mockery, for:

> The innate tortures of that deep despair,
> Which is remorse without the fear of hell,
> But is in all sufficient in itself
> Would make a hell of heaven.
>
> (III. i.)

Moreover, there is no power in a holy man that 'can exorcise

> From out the unbounded spirit that quick sense
> Of its own sins, wrongs, sufferance and revenge
> Upon itself; there is no future pang
> Can deal that justice on the self-condemn'd
> He deals on his own soul.'
>
> (Ibid.)

And it might be felt that, in the other plays, most of the main characters that perish might murmur Manfred's last words: 'Old man! 'Tis not so difficult to die,' which, Byron said, contained 'the whole effect and moral of the poem'.

'Of the poem'. And poem it is, rather than drama, a magnificent poem, rich with impassioned passages. The only human being in the whole phantasmagorical piece is the Abbot, the servants being merely stage carpentry, the Chamois Hunter as abstract as Manfred himself. The 'characters' otherwise are the spirits whom Manfred summons by his magic—the Destinies, the Spirits, Arimanes, the Witch of the Alps, and the phantom of Astarte.[1] The whole is splendidly lyrical, apart from the actual songs of the Spirits and Destinies, glowing with superb Alpine colouring in passages often versified renderings of parts of the Journal he sent to Mrs. Leigh. It is where it becomes largely 'human' drama in the last part that it falls a little flat, and we need to relish it as a poem cousin to *Queen Mab* and *Prometheus Unbound* rather than partake in it as a drama.

Many of the metaphysical themes are resumed in *Heaven and Earth*, surely one of Byron's neglected masterpieces. But this 'mystery', with all the moving qualities of a sustained narrative poem hardly comes within my scope here. *Cain* is, partly, another matter. Unactable, yes, I think. The very long duologue, the whole of Act II, between Cain and Lucifer in the unbounded regions of the illimitable and often gloomy universe would surely drive an audience to distraction or protest though it renders actual the answers to the questions raised by Manfred: What is death? And why? What is the origin of evil, and what divine justice? In common with Manfred, Cain is outraged that the Tree of Knowledge should not be the Tree of Life. Yet this mixed drama has great dramatic moments on the 'human' side, as when Cain and Adah bend over the cradle of their son Enoch, a beautifully tender scene (III.i); or the really dramatic passage, emotion fulfilling itself in action, where Cain, the live, enquiring, gentle, if rebellious being is goaded to smite his brother, by the injustice, as he sees it, of God, and by Abel's—not to say Adam's—hideous complacency. And with these comments I must leave the 'supernatural' dramas and turn to the 'human' ones.

The writing of *Manfred* evidently stirred Byron's dramatic

[1] I do not wish to enter into biographical issues. The reader may be referred to Lord Lovelace's *Astarte* (1905) and much previous and subsequent controversy.

instincts, for before it was finished he wrote to Murray for a transcript of Moore's account of the Doge Falieri, saying 'I mean to make a tragedy of the subject'. Warned by Murray of a possible parallel in *Venice Preserved*, he replied that he enormously admired Otway's play except for 'that maudlin bitch of chaste lewdness and blubbering curiosity, Belvidera, whom I utterly despise, abhor and detest'.

> But [he goes on] the story of Marino Falieri is different, and I think so much finer, that I wish Otway had taken it instead: the head conspiring against the body for a refusal of redress of a real injury . . . the devil himself could not have a finer subject, and he is your only tragic dramatist.

That was in April, 1817; but it was not until April 1820 that Byron began to write his 'historical tragedy', which occupied him for three and a half months.

Before going further into this cursory examination of Byron's plays, it might be useful to note that they all conform to a pattern set to a large degree by *Manfred*. From that poem alone we can see that, as Jeffrey said, 'his great gifts are exquisite tenderness and demoniacal sublimity'. His women, certainly, giving body to the shadow figure of Astarte, are infinitely good, almost too good to be true, devoted, gentle, yet endowed with an inner toughness of humane balance that offsets the 'demoniacal' nature of the men. The latter, because, we may think, of the Maddalo-like mood dominating Byron at this period, are all extreme, possessed, even obsessed, by one idea.

So much inadequately, for what we might call the emotional and philosophic core of Byron's dramas: what of the way the gripping ideas are given actuality? Already in *Manfred*, 'a kind of dialogue . . . or drama' we remember, we see an addiction to philosophic duologues—which in the 'human' plays often infuriatingly hold up the action—and the failure to control an impulse towards descriptive lyrical outbursts. In that poem, to be sure, the duologues are not excessively spun out, and the lyrical passages, such as the address to the sun (III. ii.), are in keeping. Yet it is disturbing suddenly to be plunged into a rhapsody on the Coliseum (III. iv.), so distant from the Alps where the play is set. This, one feels, is sheer self-indulgence on Byron's part. It is certainly magnificent, worthy of comparison with the famous stanzas in *Childe Harold*, but to obtrude it here merely distracts the reader's train of emotion.

The principles that guided Byron in constructing his dramas are indicated in his letters to Murray. Writing of *Sardanapalus* as he sent it to him, he says:

> You will find this very *un*like Shakespeare; and so much the better in one sense, for I look upon him to be the *worst* of models, though the most extraordinary of writers. It has been my object to be as simple and severe as Alfieri, and I have broken down the *poetry* as nearly I could to common language. (14 July, 1821)

And a week later: 'Mind the unities, which are my great object of research'; and he had said earlier in *Don Juan*:

> . . . as I have a high sense
> Of Aristotle and the Rules, 'tis fit
> To beg his pardon if I err a bit,
> (I. cxx.)

He was 'aware of the unpopularity of the notion' (Preface to *Sardanapalus*), but he would read the English 'a moral lesson'.

This adherence to the unities, especially of time is one of the, particularities of Byron's plays. Bishop Heber asked, if the plays were meant only to be read, what did the unities matter? But that is beside the question; for when we read we become, if we have any imagination, veritable spectators; and what causes discomfort in the reader is apt to cause failure in the theatre. The point of the unities is to avoid too far straining the sense of verisimilitude of an audience, which was Sidney's argument for respecting them; and if adherence to them

I

creates the strain, as it so often does with Byron, then their object is defeated.

Byron had not thought enough here, for structure is not so mechanical as the word might imply. It is no formal casing, but the structure of emotions built up in the spectator (or reader) as the events develop. Moreover, what is essential is variation in tension, change of pace, expectation or suspense, all the while the sense that something is happening that might have happened.

Marino Faliero opens superbly; our expectations are aroused, and almost at once we sense the hideous tension that grips the Doge as he waits to hear what sentence 'the Forty' have passed on the patrician youth, Michel Steno. But for what? An audience will want to know. A reader, possibly can wait, but in the theatre any effect must be immediate. The Doge, however, prevents his nephew Bertuccio from telling them just as he is about to do so. They will feel baffled, though readers can learn—and only then from an editor's footnote— that this outrageous young man had scribbled on the back of a chair at a Carnival festival: 'The Wife of Marino Faliero— others embrace her; he maintains her.' Without knowing this an audience will not be able to enter into the Doge's literally shattering fury when he is told that Steno, for an offence that he thinks merits death, has been sentenced merely to a month's house-arrest. And readers and audience alike only learn gradually that the Doge had married a woman young enough to be his daughter—the daughter, indeed, of his oldest friend —so they can understand the prior outburst:

> You know the full offence of this born villain,
> This creeping, coward, rank, acquitted felon,
> Who threw his sting into a poisonous libel,
> And on the honour of—oh God!—my wife.
>
> (I. ii.)

Then our bewilderment—bewilderment rather than expectation—is cleared up.

From the moment he hears the sentence the Doge becomes an obsessed person. His emotion, not the plot against Venice, is the guiding interest of the drama, and it becomes enthralling. At first he almost collapses, and has to be supported by his nephew; but when the latter offers to kill Steno, the Doge deters him. The crime is no longer his, but that of 'the Forty'. A life so vile as Steno's is 'nothing at this hour'; in the olden days 'Great Expectations had a hecatomb'. The notion brings apparent calm; he apologizes for his anger, and Bertuccio exclaims:

> Why, that's my uncle!
> The leader, and the statesman and the chief
> Of commonwealths, and sovereign of himself.
>   (I. ii.)

But the younger Faliero has hardly gone when Israel Bertuccio, chief of the arsenal, is announced; and the Doge, all too readily to carry conviction, joins in an already conveniently prepared plot to overthrow the rulers and massacre them all. This contraction of time strains our credulity: it all comes too pat. Yet as the rather lengthily protracted scene proceeds we enter into the Doge's state of mind. He has been a great soldier, defeating the 'Huns' at Zara, and a supremely successful ambassador: but on becoming Doge he has found that his power is but a pageant which he is dressed up to head, 'a thing of robes and trinkets'. The patrician government has become 'an o'ergrown aristocratic Hydra.

> The poisonous heads of whose envenom'd body
> Have breathed a pestilence upon us all'.
>   (I. ii.)

He will free Venice, avenge its wrongs, and become its acclaimed benevolent ruler. The plot, which in actual history took many months to contrive, is tied up in a twinkling. From now on, however, the Doge is torn by an inner conflict

that fascinates us. No sooner has Israel gone out than he
groans:

> At midnight. . . . I repair—
> To what? to hold a council in the dark
> With common ruffians leagued to ruin states.
>
> (I. ii.)

And at night, under the shadow of the monuments of his
ancestors, Doges also, he bursts out to Israel:

> Deem'st thou the souls of such a race as mine
> Can rest, when he, their last descendant chief,
> Stands plotting on the brink of their pure graves
> With stung plebeians?

He is 'trampling on his own affections', and when Israel asks
him, 'Do you repent?' he answers:

> No—but I *feel*, and shall do to the last.
> I cannot quench a glorious life at once,
> Nor dwindle to the thing that I must be.
>
> (III. i.)

The agony of his deed assails him later when the massacre
has been organized by the plotters. As they rejoice at the idea
of a bloody revenge for their wrongs, he implies that it is easy
for them to kill patricians, but:

> All these men were my friends: I loved them, they
> Requited honourably my regards;
> We served and fought; we smiled and wept in concert;
> We revell'd or we sorrowed side by side;
> We made alliances of blood and marriage;
> We grew in years and honours fairly . . . .
> Oime! Oime—and must I do this deed?
>
> (III. ii.)

And later in this magnificent, moving, but again too long
scene, he says:

> think not I waver;
> Ah! no; it is the *certainty* of all
> Which I must do doth make me tremble thus.

And finally, taking up a point of Israel's:

> And thou dost well to answer that it was
> 'My own free will and act', and yet you err,
> For I *will* do this! Doubt not—fear not: I
> Will be your most unmerciful accomplice!
> And yet I act no more on my free will
> Nor my own feelings—both compel me back;
> But there is *hell* within me and around,
> And like the demon who believes and trembles
> Must I abhor and do.

From that moment, I believe, a spectator would be *with* the Doge; a reader certainly is. We are on tenterhooks with him when he expects the bells of St. Mark's to toll as the signal for the rebellion to begin, a signal intolerably delayed, and then stopped when it has hardly begun. We are with him in the dignity of his last hours, when he is to be executed, and finds, like Manfred, that it is not too difficult to die; when he explains, but cannot justify his acts:

> A spark creates the flame—'tis the last drop
> Which makes the cup run o'er, and mine was full
> Already;
>
> (V. i.)

or when he says:

> And yet I find a comfort in
> The thought that these things are the work of Fate;
> For I would rather yield to gods than men.
>
> (V. ii.)

We even sympathize with his accurately prophetic curse on Venice (V. iii).

But to be at one with the hero to the extent that we can be

in the theatre is not enough, and the general conduct of the piece as a stage play, either seen or read, is a little halting. Byron is too given to long duologues, such as compose the first two acts, and the soliloquies become trying to the patience. We want to get on; we are eager to *see* what happens; when geared up to expectation we do not want to be baffled. The greatest offence in that respect in *Marino Faliero* is when Lioni, who is to be the active instrument in foiling the plot indulges in a three-page rhapsody on the beauties of Venice (IV. i). It is a fine piece of vivid descriptive poetry, but more than irrelevant, and is unnecessary either to our understanding of Lioni or to the progress of the play. Jeffrey put the objections to Byron's methods cogently enough:

> A drama is not merely a dialogue, but an *action;* and necessarily supposes that something is to pass before the eyes of the assembled spectators. . . . Its style should be calculated to excite the emotions, and keep alive the attention of gazing multitudes. (*Edinburgh Review*, xxxvi. Discussing the Preface to *Sardanapalus*.)

Drama *is* action, not merely something being talked about: and though, of course, thought promotes the action, it must be allowed time to do so. The other characters are deftly sketched in, especially Bertram, who by his humane revulsions against wholesale, indiscriminate massacre—previously revealed to us —and warning, as he thinks, one friend only, namely Lioni, betrays the traitors.

Angiolina, the Doge's young wife, is the perfect heroine of Byronic drama. Secure in herself, she wishes Steno to be left to his own shame, and when her friend Marianna says: 'Some sacrifice is due to slandered virtue', she answers, 'Why, what is virtue if it needs a victim?' We may feel that she is too absurdly innocent, for when Marianna asks her if she has never thought that some younger man might not make a better husband for her, she replies blandly:

> I knew not
> That wedded bosoms could permit themselves
> To ponder upon what they *now* might choose.
>
> (II. i.)

But this conversation gives us, for the first time in the play, some change in tension, and her succeeding dialogue with the Doge allows us to see him more three-dimensionally. On meeting her he tries for the moment to be less overwrought. 'How fares it with you?' he asks,

> . . . have you been abroad?
> The day is overcast, but the calm wave
> Favours the gondolier's light skimming oar;
> Or have you held a levee of your friends?
> Or has your music made you solitary?

But she will not be deflected. She insists on knowing what is agitating her husband who she sees to be suffering a terrible strain. And in the long duologue which follows, she, though herself magnificently proud, taxes him gently, but justly, with inordinate pride. In the final scenes, where again she is all dignity, she reveals real feeling, supporting her husband's, here, she feels, admirable pride:

> Then die, Faliero! since it must be so;
> But with the spirit of my father's friend.
> Thou has been guilty of a great offence
> Half-cancell'd by the harshness of these men.
> I would have sued to them—have pray'd to them—
> Have begged as famish'ed mendicants for bread—
> Have wept as they will cry unto their God
> For mercy, and be answer'd as they answer—
> Had it been fitting for thy name or mine . . .
>
> (V. i.)

Real feeling, yes, but no passionate love; it is patriarchal on the one hand, dutifully filial on the other. For at this stage Byron, here again reacting against the theatre of his day, would not admit passionate love as a pivot in tragedy.

But on 13th January, 1821, after talking to the Countess Guicicoli, he wrote in his Diary:

> She quarrelled with me, because I said that love was not the *loftiest* theme for true tragedy; and having the advantage of her native language, and natural female eloquence, she overcame my fewer arguments, I believe she was right. I must put more love in 'Sardanapalus'.

On that same day he wrote the opening lines of that 'tragedy'. This play, though as little written for the stage as was *Marino Faliero*, would seem far more actable. In a letter to Murray on 22nd July, telling him to print away and to publish, he said:

> I think they must own I have more *styles* than one. 'Sardanapalus' is however, almost a comic character; but for that matter, so is Richard II.

Certainly, as though Byron's self-trampling mood were for the moment assuaged, there is a much more easy flow in this play, more varied tension, than there was in the last. We come to the end of *Marino Faliero* with a real feeling of tragedy; something fine has been broken by something meaner than itself; there is in it a ritual element, the sense of sacrifice, that we get in all great tragedy. This is absent from *Sardanapalus*, which is, one might say, rather a glorious story: the holocaust that the Emperor decrees for his end is, in its way, magnificent. But do we pity? We admire, rather, him and those willing to share his fate.

On the other hand it is first-rate theatre, though not altogether free from the improbabilities that Byron flouted by his insistence on the unities, here of place, which he pushed to an extreme avoided in the other plays, so that armies do battle in a dining-room; and also to some extent of time, which compelled him to a long explanatory monologue at the outset of the play. Otherwise there is nothing to overstrain our capacity for suspension of disbelief for the moment.

Sardanapalus himself is readily understandable; he alone among Byron's heroes, though unrestrained, is not prey to an obsession. He is an extreme voluptuary, certainly, but not devoid of common sense; and this pacifist Emperor, hating bloodshed can be roused to military valour, while his final immolation on the pyre is glorious self-assertion, and no morbid death-wish, or desire for oblivion.

We can enter also into the other characters; the plain, ambitious soldier Arbaces, likable in his moment of generous gratitude, checked by the more realistic Chaldean priest, Beleses; especially we can feel for Salamenes, that alert, eminently practical servant of the state, loyal to it and to Sardanapalus, in spite of the shabby treatment dealt out to the queen, his sister. The characters are well, but not too drastically contrasted, and have in some respects so much in common as to give the plot welcome subtleties. The women compel our homage—first Myrrha, the favourite concubine, who helps to a sense of actuality the Sardanapalus whom she loves in spite of herself.

> King, I am your subject!
> Master, I am your slave! Man, I have loved you!—
> Loved you I know not by what fatal weakness,
> Although a Greek and born a foe to monarchs—
> A slave, and hating fetters—an Ionian
> And, therefore, when I love a stranger, more
> Degraded by that passion than by chains!
> Yet I have loved you. If that love were strong
> Enough to overcome all former nature,
> Shall it not claim the privilege to save you?
> (I. ii.)

Equally we can share the sentiments of the queen, whom Sardanapalus himself is forced to address as 'my gentle, wrong'd Zarina' (IV. i.). She wins not only our sympathy, but our admiration.

Nor is the increasing speed of the drama much held up by

distractingly long passages of soliloquy or speech-making, for
though these might be reduced, they aid the action of the play,
even the account Sardanapalus gives of his dream-meeting
with 'those once bloody mortals, and now bloodier idols', his
ancestors, Nimrod and Semiramis (IV. i.); or the lyrical outburst of the Hymn to the Sun, proferred by Beleses, for both
are in place as reinforcing the motives of the characters. The
duologues, again, though too long, are not merely philosophic arguments but are concerned with action, as, for instance, that between Salamenes and Sardanapalus, where the
former says:

> Think'st thou there is no tyranny but that
> Of blood and chains? The deposition of vice—
> The weakness and the wickedness of luxury—
> The negligence—the apathy—the evils
> Of sensual sloth—produce ten thousand tyrants,
> Whose delegated cruelty surpasses
> The worst acts of one energetic master
> However harsh and hard in his own bearing.
>   (I. ii.)

All this has a direct relevance to what is happening. The
emotional structure of the play, the changes in speed, the
variations in tension and expectation are admirably managed.
As Dr. Samual Chew points out in his excellent book, *Dramas
of Lord Byron*, there is a rise in the hero's fortunes, a definite
climax, a fall; the appetencies aroused are satisfied. Of its
kind, though this may not be of the highest, it is first-rate.

This was the intense period of Byron's play-writing
activities, the composition of the rest being crammed into
about six months' furious production.[1] Seeing what high
poetical power went into the 'mysteries' *Cain* and *Heaven and*

---

[1] *Marino Faliero*, begun 4 April, 1820, finished 16 July. *Sardanapalus* took
from 13 January, 1821 to 21 May; *The Two Foscari*, 12 June to 9 July; *Cain*,
begun exactly a week later, was completed on 9 September. Then, in October,
Heaven and Earth; in November (apparently), *The Deformed Transformed*, *Werner*
being begun on 18 December, and finished 20 January, 1822.

Earth, it is not surprising that the 'human' plays should fall below the previous ones in quality of thought and of workmanship.

With *The Two Foscari* we are back in Venetian history, and to obsessed characters—three of them in this play; and as Byron presents the younger Foscari he is too extreme to win our belief in his existence. There is a life only in his despair; torture is nothing to him so long as he can suffer it in Venice, and he is full of such phrases as: 'Better/Be ashes here than aught that lives elsewhere', or:

> I ask no more than a Venetian grave,
> A dungeon, what they will, so it be here
> (I. i.)

Hardly more believable is his father, the Doge, who, because he has vowed to do all that the ruling 'Ten' tell him to do, watches his son being 'put to the question': even the fiendishly revengeful hatred of Loredano, as detailed, strains our credulity. Historical? Maybe; we can read it in plain form in Rogers's *Italy*. But this does not affect an audience.

The real objection to this play is that it does not build up a satisfactory structure of the emotions. It is all one emotion of painful stress and distress, the unrelieved tension allowing hardly an instant's grace. The one moment, possibly, is when the already racked Jacopo Foscari indulges in a panegyric on his young days in Venice. Yet that passage has its own interest, for here Byron was trying to make us realize why Jacopo felt so extravagantly about Venice, compressing into a very short space what the critics of his day complained could have been convincingly led up to but for adherence to the unities. He was struggling to do what Ibsen so triumphantly achieved—abolish the first two acts of five.

If, however, the pace is too uniform, if the scene is too wholly one, made up of torture and what we might call masochistic subjection, and at the end the rapidly successive deaths of both Foscari (history again sacrificed for the sake of the unities), this is not to say that there is not some good contrast of character, such as is supplied by the ineffectual but at least humane-feeling Barbarigo who tries to make the male-volent Loredano have at least a grain of compassion: and there is Marina, the wife of Jacopo, the typical Byronic heroine, who puts up a splendid fight trying to imbue the Doge and his son with some spirit and some sense, and who, in the one really dramatic prison-scene of the play (III. i.) spiritedly stands up to Loredano. Nor is the play lacking in fine passages, and we hear echoes of plays past and to come. When the Doge speaks of

> . . . the original ordinance, that man
> Must sweat for his poor pittance
> Aloof, save fear of famine!
>
> (II. i.)

he is forestalling Cain; and when he goes on:

> All is low
> And false, and hollow—clay from first to last,
> The prince's urn no less than the potter's vessel,

and that 'nothing rests upon our will' we remember similar thoughts as uttered by Manfred and the Doge Faliero.

Of *Werner* I have neither space nor inclination to say much. It is sheer melodrama, adapted from a tale which had made a deep impression on Byron when he read it as a boy of four-teen[1], and had even then tried to dramatize. The play has certain of Byron's characteristic marks; the chief persons are, if not obsessed by an idea, at least under the ways of a passion which drives out all other thoughts. And, as usual, his main female character, Josephine, is all tender solicitude and com-mon sense. But here alone, and this is a comment on his theory, Byron sins against the sacred unities, the last act being a year later than the previous ones, and set in a different place; here

---

[1] 'Kruitzner'. The German's Tale, by Harriet Lee, in *Lee's Canterbury Tales*, which she wrote with her sister Sophia. The Lees were enormously acclaimed in their day.

alone some of Byron's characters have a certain quality of humour. But the drama seems comparatively cheap, with its somewhat tangled story, its secret passage, and its surprise when the young hero of the play, so open and daring, turns out to be the murderer when all the clues we have been given point to another as the culprit. It is mere stage trickery. That this should have been Byron's only popular success might have brought a sardonic smile to his lips. 'Just the sort of thing Drury Lane *would* like!'

Werner, however, shares with Byron's other dramas a freedom from the pseudo-Elizabethan stage diction which clogged the plays of the other poets of the time, most of whom—Coleridge, Wordsworth, Lamb, Shelley—with a notable lack of success attempted the drama, the only one approaching him in workable stage speech being Landor. Byron irritated the academic critics of his day by his free treatment of blank verse, complaining that he ended his lines too often with inexpressive words, such as 'of', 'to', 'and', 'but', 'from', and that his sole idea of blank verse was to cut up prose into sausage-lengths of ten syllables. But Byron was quite right. His verse is admirable stage speech. Dramatic blank verse is, after all, only a form which the actor can speak out effectively to a large audience, given his limited amount of breath. Byron's verse, as I hope my quotations have shown, is eminently sayable. And in 'breaking down [his] poetry as nearly as he could to common language' (he said that after *Manfred* was done) he was going back to Ben Jonson—as he did for the unities—for 'language such as men doe use'. On the whole he succeeded. As Sir Egerton Brydges wrote:

> Lord Byron's style ... did not attempt (as is the common practice) to make poetry by the metaphorical and the figurative; it followed his thoughts, and was a part of them;

and Professor Wilson Knight judges his verse as having a beautiful Augustan clarity.

He was by no means consistent—luckily, we might say. In
The Two Foscari, for example, Barbarigo can say to Loredano:

> Follow *thee*! I have follow'd long
> Thy path of desolation, as the wave
> Sweeps after that before it. . . .
>
> (I. i.)

and so on for another five lines. But *un*luckily he is given to a
conventional inversion of the negative, after the manner of
'wilt thou accept not', but without Shelley's metrical justification. In *Sardanapalus* there are such things as 'urge me not'
(I. ii) and 'Tempt me not' (II. i), where 'do not urge me', or
'do not tempt me' would do better: In *Cain* we have 'Did *I* bid
her pluck them not?' It becomes a little theatrical.

More disturbing are his lapses, which might charitably be
excused as going too far in the direction of colloquialism were
there not another explanation. Writing to Murray when
Jeffrey complained about the argument in *Cain* being to
elaborate, he riposted:

> What does Jeffrey mean by *elaborate*? Why! they were written as
> fast as I could put pen to paper, in the midst of revolutions
> and persecutions and proscriptions of all who interested me in
> Italy. They said the same of 'Lara', which I wrote while un-
> dressing, after coming home from balls and masquerades. Of all
> I have ever written, they are perhaps the most carelessly com-
> posed; and their faults, whatever they may be are those of
> negligence, and not of labour. I do not think this a merit, but
> it is a fact.
>
> (Moore's ed: XIV. 49n)

So with some of his turns of speech. It *was* negligence, and
it was *not* a merit. His abominable carelessness (one is forced to
this way of putting it), his refusal to discipline himself to the
form—and how could he have had the time for this?—led him
into unhappy phrasing. Sometimes the old gum clings to him,
as when, in *The Two Foscari* Memmo says to Marina:

> High-born dame! bethink thee
> Where thou now art.
>
> (I. i.)

a hideously stilted phrase if ever there was one—and that in the first scene, which inevitably affects the whole.

That is the worst late eighteenth-century pseudopoeticizing, and of this Byron is more often guilty than we would wish. Sometimes he goes too far in the other direction, that of slack everyday speech. For example, in *Marino Faliero*, just after the Doge hears the shattering news that the youth who has insulted him, and the Ducal crown, and his wife, has received a trivial sentence, and he is so faint that he has to clutch at his nephew for support, the latter says, 'Nay Cheer up, be calm' (I. ii): we are no longer in the Doge's palace but in the pub next door, and in *Werner*, in the admirably dramatic scene (V. i) where Siegendorf, once Werner, is talking to Gabor, the supposed murderer of Strahlenheim, we get:

> *Gabor:* Allow me to enquire who profited
> By Strathlenheim's death? Was't I—as poor as ever;
> And poorer by suspicion on my name!
> The baron lost in that last outrage neither
> Jewels nor gold; his life alone was sought,—
> A life which stood between the claims of others
> To honours and estates scarce less than princely.
> *Siegendorf:* These hints, as vague as vain, attach no less
> To me than to my son.
> *Gabor:*   I can't help that . . .
>
> (V. i.)

The phrase comes too bluntly after the excellently running stage speech that Byron wrote on either side of it. The ethos of the scene is almost destroyed.

Yet, however much we may admit flaws in Bryon's dramas, we are compelled to recognize them as products of a great spirit, undergoing, beneath the careless life that all could see, grievous distress, realizing piercingly, as Maddalo did, that

> Most wretched men
> Are cradled into poetry by wrong,
> They learn in suffering what they teach in song.
> (*Julian and Maddalo* 11. 544-6.)

They are certainly among Byron's most deeply inspired creations. All of them, even those I have barely touched on, have tremendous passages, and it would seem monstrous that we should be debarred from seeing them in the theatre.

For though they were not meant for the stage, we can ask ourselves whether we would not experience in the theatre a greatly heightened sense of the actuality of what Byron was, not so much presenting, as asking us to read about. Unfortunately, contemptuous of the theatre, writing for the study, and thus not needing to bend himself to the exigencies of the medium he despised, he allowed himself freedoms to which a reader *can* adjust himself, but which would be fatal on the stage.

Yet I feel strongly that, impertinent though it might be, Byron's dramas could be made viable as stage plays. Adaptation would certainly be required—Bertuccio Faliero ought to be allowed to tell the audience what was the crime that outraged the Doge—but the main task would be to cut, sometimes ruthlessly. The monologues could certainly be reduced, and the duologues imperatively must be, for drama seldom results when only two people are in action. There is not enough clash, and the best scenes in both *Marino Faliero* and *Sardanapalus* are those when several persons are in *action*. For, to repeat, drama *is* action, and not 'a kind of poem in dialogue'. Further when several persons have to be told separately of the hero's state of mind, the repetition, already a trifle tedious in the reading, would be irritating in the theatre. We read again and again how Marino Faliero defeated the Huns at Zara: again and again we learn that to be a Doge is nothing, that indeed

There is no such thing—.
It is a word—nay, worse—a worthless by-word,
The most despised, wrong'd, outraged, helpless wretch . . .

(I. ii.)

For the reader this may possibly intensify the Doge's agony;
but an audience is impatient at hearing the same thing over
and over.

So the plays as they stand, with the possible exception of
Sardanapalus, may well seem intractable to the manager of
a theatre. Yet they are so deeply felt, so full of impassioned
life, that it should be possible to make sure of tedium never
overtaking an audience, and, without distortion, make superb
stage productions of these dramas. It would take thought,
and real sympathy with what Byron wished to convey, but
the labour would be a thousand times worthwhile. If ever the
dream of a national theatre is realized, the plays of Byron
ought, surely, to form a not inglorious part of the extra-
Shakespearean repertory.

WILLIAM HAZLITT*

> Both from disposition and habit, I can *assume* nothing in
> word, look, or manner. I cannot steal a march upon public
> opinion in any way. . . . I neglect [the] ordinary means of re-
> commending myself to the good graces and admiration of
> strangers (and, as it appears, even of philosophers and friends).
> ('A Farewell to Essay-Writing'. *Winterslow*.)

HAZLITT, in fact, was an awkward customer. Talfourd and
Coleridge agree in their description of his ungainly appearance, his boorishness, ascribing these social defects to intense shyness. 'His bashfulness was almost painful', Talfourd
says; but when with friends, especially with Lamb, he could
talk fascinatingly. And even if, according to Coleridge, 'he
delivers himself of almost all his conceptions with a Forceps,
yet he says more than any man I ever knew that is his own way
of his own' (to Thomas Wedgwood, 16 September, 1803).

He wouldn't fit in; he could never belong to any literary
clique or movement, and that is what still makes him an
awkward customer, for now he doesn't fit in with the common
conception of the Romantic Revival (in any case an absurd
misnomer). Only in one respect does he seem to belong,
namely in the immense enthusiasm that greeted the French
Revolution, which occurred when he was a boy: here he is
with Wordsworth, Coleridge and Southey, and all the rest.
The difference is that the splendid idea was always in his mind;
all his life he was a passionate admirer of Napoleon, and he

* Reprinted from *Review of English Literature*, Vol. II, no. 1, 1961. by
permission of Longmans, Green & Co., Ltd and the British Council.

never forgave the others for, as we might put it, ratting. *He* would never turn Tory. It is this independence of opinion, this refusal to be carried away by those of others, that makes him valuable to us now, as, apart from anything else, preventing us from falling into the common error of regarding the Romantic movement as a triumphant tide that swept everything before it.

One can see why he was unpopular. However much he might like or admire a man, when he discussed him he was not content to tell the truth and nothing but the truth about him, he would always tell the whole truth. That is why, more than from any other writer of his day, we get the sense of the time as a whole, and not from some theoretical point of view. Reading, say, 'My First Acquaintance with Poets' or 'On the Conversation of Poets', we get a vivid sense of the people as such, of how they moved and talked. Independent though he is, he is not at all egotistical, nor puffed up about his unique merits; he is content to live to himself.

> What I mean by living to one's-self is living in the world, as in it, not of it: it is as if no one knew there was such a person, and you wished no one to know it: it is to be a spectator of the mighty scene of things . . . to take a thoughtful, anxious interest in what is passing in the world, but not to feel the slightest inclination to make or meddle with it.
>
> ('On Living to One's-Self'. *Table Talk.*)

It was this attitude that enabled him to achieve that centrality of mind that makes him so useful, so sane, so discriminating a commentator upon literature.

A commentator rather than what we nowadays call a critic; and a brilliant one, for:

> He was, in the truest sense, a man of original mind; that is, he had the power of looking at things for himself, or as they really were, instead of blindly trusting to, and fondly repeating what others told him what they were. He got rid of the go-cart of prejudice and affectation, with the learned lumber that follows at

their heels, because he could do without them. . . . He was neither a pedant nor a bigot. . . . In treating of men and manners, he spoke of them as he found them, not according to preconceived notions and abstract dogmas. . . . In criticising books he did not compare them with rules and systems, but told us what he saw to like or dislike in them.

That extract is not from an essay on Hazlitt, as it might fittingly be, but part of what he himself wrote about Montaigne ('The Periodical Essayists', *The English Comic Writers*). For he was no theorist, no elaborator of systems; he had 'no fangs for recondite research'. In considering any work, whether of literature or painting, he asked, 'What does this mean for me, do for me?': for though he paid tribute to Schlegel for his work on Shakespeare, he was free of the Teutonic disease of distorting everything through transcendental or categorical lenses. He lived the literature that he read, tasting it fully, relating it to his experience as the whole man that he was. Take the opening lecture *On the English Poets*, 'On Poetry in General', an essay at once brilliant and solid:

> Impassioned poetry is an emanation of the total and intellectual part of our nature, as well as of the sensitive—of the desire to know, the will to act, and the power to feel; and ought to appeal to those different parts of our constitution, in order to be perfect.

Or, a little later, where he touches on what we have come to call 'the objective co-relative':

> Poetry is the highest eloquence of passion, the most vivid form of expression that can be given to our conception of any thing, whether pleasurable or painful, mean or dignified, delightful or distressing. It is the perfect coincidence of the image and the words with the feeling we have, which we cannot get rid of in any other way, that gives an instant 'satisfaction to the thought'.

This is all an appeal to experience, to the sense common to all

of us: there are no Sidneyan showers of sweet discourse, no
pretence that the poet is the unacknowledged legislator of the
world, not even the more modest claims of the Preface to
Lyrical Ballads. What he looks for are words and sentiments
that 'come home to the bosoms and businesses of men' (he
was as fond of using that tag from Bacon as Bagehot—who in
many way resembles him—was to be); and he does not mind
where, or in what form he finds it. He is no fastidious
excluder, thinking that because one thing is good another must
be bad. In 'A Farewell to Essay-Writing' he tells of how,
after a walk in his beloved country, something having reminded him of Dryden's *Theodore and Honoria:*

> I return home resolved to read the entire poem through, and,
> after dinner, drawing my chair to the fire, and holding a small
> print close to my eyes, launch into the full tide of Dryden's
> couplets (a stream of sound), comparing his didactic and des-
> criptive pomp with the simple pathos and picturesque truth of
> Boccaccio's story, . . .

Hazlitt could taste both dishes with equal relish.

That is why he is so sound a guide as an appreciator, if you
wish to deny the name of critic to a man who can respond to so
many imaginative delights, knowing what he likes, and, more
importantly, why. Take some of the lectures on poetry, where
he preferred to pair poets, so as to contrast their flavours,
though he does not deny himself discursive comments on
other poets of the same time. A good example is his lecture on
'Dryden and Pope', in which, incidentally there is very little
on Dryden to whom he refers mainly to show—and how well
he does it!—in what way he differs from Pope. Pope he places
in the front rank of the poets of art rather than of nature, and
therefore deserving of a place above the second-raters in the
latter class. 'Young . . . Gray, or Akenside, only follow in the
train of Milton and Shakespeare: Pope and Dryden walk by
their side, though of an unequal stature, and are entitled to a
first place in the lists of fame'. He is acutely aware of Pope's

limitations, but can thoroughly enter into a delighted ap-
praisal of his qualities, as he felt them. After quoting the end
of the 'Epistle to Jervas', he bursts out: 'And shall we cut
ourselves off from beauties like these with a theory?' Similarly,
in discussing 'Thomson and Cowper'—a lecture which, it
might be remarked, should, if read, dispel the silly theory one
still hears bleated at intervals, that Wordsworth discovered
nature—he beautifully distinguishes their qualities, and the way
they feel nature. There are some remarks, too, on Crabbe, who
'describes the interior of a cottage like a person sent there to
distrain for rent'. The lecture closes with some quotations
from Wordsworth. Or, to take another kind of instance,
though as a painter what he most admired about Spenser was
his pictorial quality, he does not ignore other aspects. 'People',
he says, 'are afraid of the allegory, as if they thought it would
bite them.'

It was this even temper that enabled Hazlitt to welcome the
work of his contemporaries, whether or no he admired them
personally. He was the first popular writer to do justice to
Wordsworth. Though he disliked him intensely, repelled by
his monstrous egotism (as comes out again and again), he
praised him highly, both in these lectures and in *The Spirit of
the Age*, as 'the most original poet now living'. In the earlier
essay he says:

> Of many of the Lyrical Ballads it is impossible to speak in
> terms of too high praise, such as [he names a few] and a hun-
> dred others of inconceivable beauty, of perfect originality and
> pathos. They open a finer and deeper vein of feeling than any
> poet in modern times has done or attempted.

The later one contains as much praise, but is tempered by
severe criticism of Wordsworth's narrowness of sympathy; he
remarks *en passant:*

> We do not think our author has any very cordial sympathy
> with Shakespear. How should he? Shakespear was the least of
> an egotist of any body in the world.

It was, in part, this capacity for detachment that lost him his friends—except for Lamb—and this capacity may in some degree have been a result of lost illusions, a refusal to compromise. He would not steal a march upon public opinion in any way, nor upon private. His greatest disappointment was Coleridge, leaving aside the blighting of revolutionary hopes. One thinks of his superb description of Coleridge in 'My First Acquaintance with Poets', or of a passage in 'On Going a Journey', the recognition of real genius coming in his lecture on 'The Living Poets':

> . . . I may say of him here, that he is the only person I ever knew who answered to the idea of a man of genius. He is the only person from whom I ever learnt anything. . . . His genius at that time had angelic wings, and fed on manna. He talked on for ever; and you wished him to talk on for ever. . . .

And so on. But then we come to *The Spirit of the Age*, and Hazlitt sums up the waste of this genius, in talk rather than in writing; how Coleridge busied himself with 'vibrations and vibratiuncules', how he 'lost himself in the labyrinths of the Hartz Forest and the Kantean philosophy, and amongst the cabalistic names of Fichte and Schelling and Lessing and God knows who'. There follows the cry of pain:

> Alas! 'Frailty, thy name is *Genius!*'—What is become of all this mighty heap of hope, of thought, of learning and humanity? It has ended in swallowing doses of oblivion and in writing paragraphs in the *Courier*. Such and so little is the mind of man!

Yet if Coleridge, abandoning 'Liberty (the philosopher's and the poet's bride) had fallen a victim . . . to the murderous practices of the hag Legitimacy,' at least he had not, like Southey, allowed himself to be trammelled into a poet laureate, or, like Wordsworth, into a stamp-distributor. How the old dream, including the fantasy of Pantisocracy, had vanished!

Luckily, with men of long ago, such considerations are out: Shakespeare is removed from all these battles. And how wholesome to go back to Hazlitt on Shakespeare after reading the erudite wisdom of modern commentators, each determined to make Shakespeare the prophet of what he will, each striving to discover what, more likely than not, was never there. Shakespeare, for Hazlitt, was not a man of genius to be pondered in the study, but to be encountered on the stage. (One suggests, hesitantly, that Shakespeare might rather have liked that.) He takes it that Shakespeare meant his people to mean what a spectator of his plays might suppose them to mean; Troilus is a lover, not a kind of F. H. Bradley worrying about the nature of reality. For him Shakespeare was above all a man who loved human beings for what they were, not as pegs upon which to hang some morality or other. So in the essay on *Measure for Measure*, 'a play as full of genius as it is of wisdom', we read:

> Shakespeare was in one sense the least moral of writers; for morality (commonly so called) is made up of antipathies; and his talent consisted in sympathy with human nature, in all its shapes, degrees, depressions and elevations. . . . In one sense he was no moralist at all; in another he was the greatest of all moralists. He was a moralist in the sense that nature is one.

Here De Quincey is in line with him, saying in his essay on Pope: 'Poetry . . . can teach only as nature teaches, as forests teach, as the sea teaches, viz., by deep impulse, by hieroglyphic suggestion'.

And as we read Hazlitt on Shakespeare we may feel how refreshing it is to escape from the fascinating webs woven round him for us by modern commentators, as Hazlitt escaped from those of his day.

Maybe Mr. J. B. Priestley is right when in his recent finely appreciative pamphlet (in the Writers and their Work Series), he prefers to call Hazlitt an essayist rather than a critic. You may, it is true, not go very deep with him as a critic, but you cannot go wrong. Certainly as an essayist he is invigorating to read, if only for the vitality of the language which so well expresses the virility of his being. And again, when writing of Montaigne, the words are applicable to him—'no juggling tricks or solemn mouthing, no laboured attempts at proving himself always in the right, and everybody else in the wrong', except, so far as the last statement goes, when he is furiously fighting his attackers, as in the splendid invective of *A Letter to William Gifford, Esq*. He worked hard to evolve his manner of writing, which is a model of what such writing ought to be, 'concrete, vivid, personal, vigorous', as W. D. Howe put it. It is concise without being terse, save when he wants it to be so; a great admirer of Burke's writings, he had no objection to eloquence. He achieved this, however, by the use of the right word, not by being inflated. 'I hate to see a load of bandboxes go along the street, and I hate to see a parcel of big words without anything in them.'

Thus he can be dexterously incisive, as when he tells Gifford: 'But you are a nuisance, and ought to be abated.' Or in that splendidly modulated passage on Bentham in *The Spirit of the Age*, when he says: 'He turns wooden utensils in a lathe for exercise, and fancies he can turn men in the same manner.' That he thought about prose a good deal is plain from the admirable criticisms of Addison in 'On the Prose Style of Poets', of Johnson in 'The Periodical Essayists' (*The English Comic Writers*), apart from the disquisition 'On Familiar Style' (*Table Talk*). He abominated jargon of any kind, or any pretentiousness. He is infinitely readable. True, he sometimes goes on too long, makes his point too often; he quotes too much. But he is full of delightful surprises. Who would expect to find in the description of Cavanagh, the fives-player, such a delightful jump as 'His blows were not undecided and ineffectual—lumbering like Mr. Wordsworth's epic poetry, nor wavering like Mr. Coleridge's lyric prose, nor short of the mark like Mr. Brougham's speeches, nor wide of it like Mr.

Canning's wit, nor foul like the Quarterly, nor *let* balls like the Edinburgh Review' ('The Indian Jugglers', *Table Talk*). He is enormously varied in his subjects; he can be brilliantly descriptive as in his account of a boxing match ('The Fight'); he is full of common sense and citizen-like acumen in his essays on public affairs, he is penetrating in his character studies, revealing of ourselves in the essays that deal with what we might call general psychology. And for those of us who pretend to be critics, the chapter 'On Criticism' should be a stimulating as well as a salutary discipline.

WALTER SAVAGE LANDOR

*His Prose**

THE fate which has overtaken Landor would not be altogether to his liking. That he should not be widely read would gratify him; his readers all know the proud 'I will dine late but the dining-room will be well lighted, the guests few and select'; what might ruffle him is the indiscriminate praise of some of his admirers, and the unlucky selections of the anthologists. The compliment he would most appreciate would be such treatment as he gave to Milton, who called forth his warmest admiration—namely, a meticulous weeding out of the tares from the corn, since it is only rich fields that do not look barren after the process. The common sense of such a way of getting to work he upholds in a letter written by Aspasia to Cleone:

> Myrtis and Corinna have no need of me. To read and re-commend their works, to point out their beauties and defects, is praise enough.
>
> 'How!' methinks you exclaim. 'To point out defects! is that praising?'
>
> Yes, Cleone; if with equal good faith and accuracy you point out their beauties too. It is only thus a fair estimate can be made; and it is only by such fair estimate that a writer can be exalted to his proper station. If you toss up the scale too high it descends again rapidly below its equipose; what it contains drops out, and people catch at it, scatter it, and lose it.

* Based on an article which first appeared in *The Times Literary Supplement*, 19, July, 1928; reprinted by kind permission of the Editor.

Yet to apply such a method to Landor would be not only a labour of love, but an occupation of years, especially if it were hoped to reach near his own ideal standard as stated in the 'Conversation' between Alfieri and Salomon:

> A perfect piece of criticism must exhibit where a work is good or bad; why it is good or bad; in what degree it is good or bad; must also demonstrate in what manner and to what extent the same ideas or reflections have come to others, and, if they be clothed in poetry, why, by an apparently slight variation, what in one author is mediocrity, in another is excellence.

The first problem which confronts the critic is to discover what it is that Landor stands for, where to place him in the line of literary or social tradition. Here is a man who, on the one hand, had met Addison's daughter, and to whom, on the other, Swinburne dedicated *Atalanta in Calydon*. What, thus linked with two ages and dwelling in an intermediate one, does this man represent? The answer is harder to find for him than for any other writer. Not that he is indefinite, far from it, but he is so bafflingly varied. A few passages may show the difficulty:

> LEONTION: (to Epicurus): Although you teach us the necessity of laying a strong hand on the strong affections, you never pull one feather from the wing of Love.
> EPICURUS: I am not so irreligious.
> TERMISSA: I think he could only twitch it just enough to make the gentle god turn round, and smile on him.
> LEONTION: You know little about the matter, but may live to know all. Whatever we may talk of torments, as some do, there must surely be more pleasure in desiring and not possessing, than in possessing and not desiring.
> EPICURUS: Perhaps so: but consult the intelligent. Certainly there is a middle state between love and friendship, more delightful than either, but more difficult to remain in.

The last sentence may be pure Landor, but the note struck
before it, and struck in more than one conversation, is a note
often heard in the seventeenth century, in Suckling, and Cow-
ley, and Congreve, the 'against fruition' note, the fear of disillusion. Of course, it is dangerous, as he warned us, to attribute to him the opinions of his characters; yet there are some
of his persons whom he seems to have chosen to express his
own thoughts, such as Epicurus, and in part Porson. Thus,
from some of his other utterances, we are tempted to regard
him as his own Lucian, and here he speaks pure Voltairean
eighteenth century:

> We are on earth to learn what can be learnt upon earth, and
> not to speculate on what can never be. . . . Let men learn
> what benefits men; above all things to contract their wishes, to
> calm their passions, and, more especially, to dispel their fears.
> Now these are to be dispelled, not by collecting clouds, but by
> piercing and scattering them. . . . Much of what we call sublime
> is only the residue of infancy, and the worst of it.

Indeed, if he belongs to any race at all, it is to that remnant
of the eighteenth century, rugged and extravagant, wilful and
reckless, which strayed into the nineteenth, of whom Osbalde-
stone, in another sphere, is a typical example. If he is nineteenth century also—and again and again, especially in his
attitude towards the emotions, he reminds us that he is so—
it is with a difference. Lord Normanby, in the conversation
between the Duc de Richelieu and others, would not altogether have earned the approbation either of Dickens or of
Matthew Arnold, since there is something withheld just where
they would have been most prepared to give:

> Magnitude and power are sublime but in the second degree,
> managed as they may be. Where the heart is not shaken, the
> gods thunder and stride in vain. True sublimity is the per-
> fection of the pathetic, which has other sources than pity:
> generosity, for instance, and self-devotion. When the generous
> and self-devoted man suffers, there comes pity: the basis of

the sublime is above the water, and the poet, with or without the gods, can elevate it above the skies. Terror is but the relic of a childish feeling: pity is not given to children.

Finally, here and there, especially in his verse, we seem to get hints of a feeling which became more important after his death than it was in his own day, and we are sometimes reminded of Hardy:

> I led him to Bellagio, of earth's gems
> The brightest.
>   We in England have as bright,
> Said he, and turned his face towards the west.
> I fancied in his eyes there was a tear,
> I know there was in mine; we both stood still.

It is not so much the actual versification, as the approach, which is like Hardy's, what he was trying to make his poetry do. We must conclude then, that unlike most of his contemporaries, Byron, for instance, he stands not for a movement nor for an age, but for a definite quality which may in the best sense be called classical, for an attitude towards life which, though it may be distinguished from the romantic by its desire for balance and control, is still more distinguished from it by its refusal to compromise with what it considers pernicious—namely, desire which takes no cognizance of facts. The basis of all great writing is romantic, but the unredeemed romantic writer gives emotion a value according to its strength: the classical writer, ordering his forces, values it by virtue of its direction. Landor, to use one of his own phrases, had this of god-like in him, a love of order, and the power of bringing great things into it.

Certainly if we accept T. E. Hulme's definition of the romantic as one who does not believe in the fall of man, Landor was no romantic; he felt strongly that it was necessary for man to assert himself, to achieve some definite form. But indeed, his romanticism is not that of his age; it is, rather, like that of Dryden, whom in many ways he resembles—in his unquestioning acceptance of the value of art and especially of literature; in his preoccupation with language and his desire to improve the instrument; and, as far as tastes go, in his love of Chaucer. In proof, we need only read his words on Dryden, and see how applicable they are to the writer of them. Talking of Cowper, Porson remarks:

> Dryden possesses a much richer store of thoughts, expatiates upon more topics, has more vigour, vivacity, and animation. He is always shrewd and penetrating, explicit and perspicuous, concise where conciseness is desirable, and copious where copiousness can yield delight. When he aims at what is highest in poetry, the dramatic, he falls below his 'Fables'.

Substitute 'Conversations' for 'Fables' and the judgment is true of Landor, though his plays are by no means despicable. But he is most like Dryden in that kind of romanticism which asks for the big subject to mould, which, confident of its powers, demands the large canvas, and stretches out beyond the grand manner to the sublime. 'Gebir', published in the same year as 'Lyrical Ballads', outdoes in the trappings of romance all that the romantics were to do until Shelley, or, one might even say, until 'Hyperion'. It dazzles with its movement and its colour, its disturbing leaps, its ornament, and its implication of the light that never was on sea or land. Yet even there Landor always has his eye on fact; metaphor does not outstrip its bounds to become preachment or prophecy.

No clearer instance, perhaps, can be found than the famous lines about the shell, of which Wordsworth in 'The Excursion' used—Landor always thought he took—the idea. Landor is, as usual, compact:

> But I have sinuous shells of pearly hue. . . .
> Shake one, and it awakens, then apply
> Its polished lips to your attentive ear,
> And it remembers its august abodes
> And murmurs as the ocean murmurs there.

Wordsworth's version, in Landor's phrase, is 'incrusted with a compost of mucus and shingle':

> I have seen
> A curious child, who dwelt upon a tract
> Of inland ground, applying to his ear
> The convolutions of a smooth-lipped shell;
> To which, in silence hushed, his very soul
> Listened intensely; and his countenance soon
> Brightened with joy; for from within were heard
> Murmurings, whereby the monitor expressed
> Mysterious union with its native sea.
> Even such a shell the universe itself
> Is to the ear of Faith; and there are times.
> I doubt not, when to you it doth impart
> Authentic tidings of invisible things. . . .

And so it goes on, Wordsworth's desire being not to actualize experience, but to make an object a starting-point for an experience. The contrast with Wordsworth is worth dwelling on; for, as he was the poet most opposite to Landor, more of the latter's poetic faith is probably to be learnt from his criticisms of Wordsworth, in the two admirable conversations between Southey and Porson, than in any other of his writings. His first complaint is that Wordsworth shows himself too much in his poetry, whereas a work should have impersonality: Greek poets were hid, 'Mr. Wordsworth, on the contrary, strokes down his waistcoat, hems gently first, then hoarsely, then impatiently, rapidly, and loudly. You turn your eyes, and see more of the showman than of the show.' The second complaint, of more general application, is that the didactics are too blatant, metaphysics too often a mere refuge from that clear thinking which alone can produce clear poetry.

> You talk of philosophy (it is again Porson who speaks), and in poetry let it exist; but let its vein run through a poem as our veins run through the body, and never be too apparent; for the prominence of veins, in both alike, is a symptom of weakness, feverishness, and senility.

A further cause of objection was an unclassical diffuseness, 'often the weakness of vanity', since, the word is with Porson still, 'The poetical form, like the human, to be beautiful, must be succinct. When we grow corpulent we are said to lose our figure'. Landor was to praise Wordsworth generously in his later conversation with Archdeacon Hare, but his poetic faith remained the same from the time he published his first verses, in 1795, to the time when he laid down his pen in 1864.

His own verse, then, is 'diaphanous', to use the term which he opposed to the 'prismatic' nature of the verse of his contemporaries; he did not want the flashing facets so much as clear depth. His own best things are those which are clear and hard as gems, complete objects in themselves, but they do not glint; they are transparent. Swinburne thought 'the very brightest of all the jewels in Landor's crown of song' the lines:

> Stand close around, ye Stygian set,
>   With Dirce in one boat conveyed!
> Or Charon, seeing, may forget
>   That he is old, and she a shade,

while to others the well-known 'Rose Aylmer' will claim pride of place, or one of the hundred and forty odd, no less, Ianthe poems, written for the Comtesse de Molandé. But great concentration of passion must go to make lambent a very concentrated manner, otherwise a toy is the result; and with Landor one often feels a little uneasy, as though, immaculately simple as his words are, the spirit of the conceit had crept into his form: it is the skill we are astonished at. He is happiest in the rather longer poems, where his exquisite tenderness can have the room it needs without that wide compass which sometimes trapped him into sentimentality:

> Ternissa, you are fled!
>   I say not to the dead,
> But to the happy ones who rest below:

L

For surely, surely, where
   Your voice and graces are,
Nothing of death can any feel or know.
   Girls who delight to dwell
   Where grows most asphodel,
Gather to their calm breasts each word you speak:
   The mild Persephone
   Places you on her knee.
And your cool palm smooths down stern Pluto's cheek.

His longer poems in the 'Hellenics' are undoubtedly well done; they are charming and graceful, close-knit and 'diaphanous', but they have not the ringing note of thoughts conceived as emotions. His own phrase, quoted earlier, of thoughts being clothed in poetry gives a clue as to why this is so. Poetry is not thought clothed in an especial kind of diction; the thought does not precede the words, it is contemporaneous with them; it springs to life in the image, as, indeed, is sometimes the case in the 'Hellenics,' as in the ending of 'Corythos I':

     . . . 'What open brows
The brave and beauteous ever have!' said she,
'But even the hardiest, when above their heads
Death is impending, shudder at the sight
Of barrows on the sands and bones exposed
And whitening in the wind, and cypresses
From Ida waiting for dissever'd friends.'

But good as Landor's poems often are, and some, in their sphere, unmatchable, there can be no doubt that he was really more at his ease in prose than in verse, especially in that form of prose which has the quality of poetry in so far as it depends for its effect, not upon logical structure but upon spontaneous imagery. A comparison may here be apposite of the two forms of the same passage, the dialogue between Peleus and Thetis which appears as verse in the 'Hellenics' and as prose in the superb 'Conversation' between Epicurus, Leontion and Ternissa. One short speech must suffice:

> Smile thus, smile thus anew. Ages shall fly
> Over my tomb while thou art flourishing
> In youth eternal, the desire of Gods,
> The light of Ocean to its lowest deep.
> The inspirer and sustainer here on earth
> Of ever-flowing song.

Smile thus! Oh smile anew and forget thy sorrows. Ages shall fly over my tomb, while thou art flourishing in imperishable youth, the desire of Gods, the light of the depths of Ocean, the inspirer and sustainer of ever-flowing song.

The rhythm of the prose piece is surer, the words themselves more precise—how much better 'imperishable' is than 'eternal'—and the verse, though less here than in the immediately preceding piece, gives a sense of being padded. What, for instance, is the object of 'here on earth'? The poetry, instead of being more concentrated than the prose, is less so: it is, in short, versified prose: it is more prosaic.

Thus, although it has been claimed that Landor will live by his verse rather than by his prose, it is plausible to maintain the opposite view. The long series of 'Imaginary Conversations' are more than what Landor hoped they would be, a piece of solid history; they are an inexhaustible source of delight. If he opened no new windows upon reality, he freshened the fields in which human sympathies dwell, and in this way broadened the basis of our experience. Seeing no essential difference between past and present either in politics or in letters, he transfused the problems and passions of his day into the times that had been. He did not bring the past into the present as the dramatist does, nor take himself to the past as the historian may do, but he bodily transported his time along the centuries so that Lucian speaking with Timotheus is merely the Duke of Wellington arguing with Sir Robert Inglis. In either case the subject is the same, the intolerance of Christianity towards a humane religion it hopes to displace; and, if the drawing of the picture is different, this is merely to suit the frame; the identical colours are used. In the same way the conversation of the Ciceros might well be one between Sir Austen and Mr. Neville Chamberlain—though there the colouring would have been different—while Epicurus and Menander are but Southey and Porson arguing on a different theme. We feel the same blood flowing through the ages, so that the experience of the past is bestowed upon the present, not that idle experience which is garnered in books and laid for reference upon the study shelf, but an experience of being in which we ourselves are involved, and which enriches us. Landor offers life with both hands, but because he is proud, there are not many readers, as readers go, who have yet gone forward to accept the gift.

He said of himself that he would never be popular, nor did he really wish it, for, like all aristocratic republicans, he hated the mob; and the opinion has been so often repeated that Mr. Saintsbury has warned us against ever saying it again. But if it is true, it is the business of the critic to discover why it is so. Nor is this easy. To all appearance there is something in his works for every taste. There are, of course, those discussions of language, as in the dialogue between Dr. Johnson and Horne Tooke, or the one on Plato's Greek between Chesterfield and Chatham, which will turn away all except the enthusiast for literature; just as many passages of abstruse classical reference both in his verse and prose will discourage all except the scholar or the professed Landorian. Nor will the common reader be drawn to that superb criticism of Milton in the Landor-Southey conversations. Never was criticism at once so profound and so gay, so devoted to its object yet so free of any taint of the study. But if these things will appeal only to especial groups, Landor, on the other hand, produced a vast gallery of portraits, rich and varied in colouring, masterly in drawing. There is generous indignation in some, in the one

with Queen Pomare, for instance, which is turned to satire and
irony in others, as in the dialogue between Pitt and Canning;
sheer fun in two or three, as when the great Duke amuses himself hugely at the expense of Sir Robert Inglis; there is story-
telling with Boccaccio, dramatic episode with Admiral Blake,
with Cromwell, and with Addison. But above all there are the
delicious backwaters of quietude to be found not only in the
classical dialogues, where they most abound—in 'Aesop and
Rhodope', in 'Epicurus, Leontion and Ternissa'—but also in
such things as 'Walton, Cotton and Oldways', where Landor
put all the fruit of meditation proper to a rich and powerful
nature, and where he exhibits the warm feelings common to
mankind, even sometimes with too little restraint. What can
be lacking, from the point of view of the ordinary reader, in
the following passage from the dialogue of the Ciceros?

> The Gods, who have given us our affections, permit us
> surely the use and the signs of them. Immoderate grief, like
> everything else immoderate, is useless and pernicious; but if we
> did not tolerate and endure it, if we did not even cherish it in its
> season, much of what is best in our faculties, much of our
> tenderness, much of our generosity, much of our patriotism,
> much also of our genius, would be stifled and extinguished.
>
> When I hear any call upon another to be manly and to res-
> train his tears, if they flow from the social and the kind affect-
> ions, I doubt the humanity and distrust the wisdom of the
> counsellor. Were he humane, he would be more inclined to pity
> and to sympathize than to lecture and reprove; and were he
> wise, he would consider that tears are given us by Nature as a
> remedy to affliction, although, like other remedies, they should
> come to our relief in private.

But even there the ordinary reader may scent just what he
most dislikes, a certain aloofness. This, in part, is principle:

> For any high or any wide operation, a poet must be endued,
> not with passion indeed, but with power and mastery over it;
> with imagination and reflection, with observation, and with

discernment. . . . Homer in himself is subject to none of the
passions; but he sends them all forth on his errands, with as
much precision and velocity as Apollo his golden arrows. The
hostile Gods, the very Fates themselves, must have wept with
Priam in the tent before Achilles: Homer stands unmoved.

Moreover, beyond this there is another kind of more
personal aloofness which may be felt in Landor's work, for,
passionate as he was in many ways, his is the passion of an individual and not the common passion. At school and university he would never compete for a prize, though renowned
as the best Latinist in any gathering. Like his own Porson, he
'always avoided, with timid prudence, the bird-cage walk of
literature'. But this meritorious isolation has its dangers,
especially for a man already so idiosyncratic as Landor; it leads
to crankiness, and the reader at once sees this in his freaks of
spelling, such as 'forener' for 'foreigner', and in his continued
use of hath and doth. The dialogue form is itself not popular,
and when in it the writer, while sailing along comfortably in
pleasant conversation, suddenly obtrudes political dogmas,
introduces a piercing piece of literary criticism, launches out
into a diatribe against priests, or, again, without apparent
connexion abuses Plato, the reader is too much disconcerted.
Indeed, the delightfulness of Landor is in virtues which the
literary man will appreciate, rather than the common reader;
and here again he is like Dryden.

Besides, if Landor moves and interests and excites by
means of the great thoughts he occasionally strikes out,
though he was not a great thinker: if as often as not he appeals
to the general stock of experience and feeling, it is really the
quality of his prose which makes his work so reliable a
pleasure. Of his copiousness examples have been given; of his
conciseness it is equally easy to find instance. Take the remark
on Theophrastus made by Epicurus: 'He has one great merit in
style: he is select and sparing in the use of metaphors: that
man sees badly who sees everything double.' The quotation

leads one to note another great merit in him: how in his detailed criticism he always strikes out some general truth, the one cited being the most appropriate instrument for testing much of the more pretentious writing of today. He can manage the epigram, the aphoristic remark, better than any one since Halifax, but he never allows it to weary. How well he can manage the long sentence, allowing it to swell and grow, and then discipline it with a taut rhythm at the end, may be illustrated by a speech of Sidney's to Brooke:

> Greville! Greville! it is better to suffer than to lose the power of suffering. The perception of beauty, grace, and virtue is not granted to all alike. There are more who are contented with an ignoble union on the flat beaten earth before us, than there are who, equally disregarding both unfavourable and favourable clamours, make for themselves room to stand on an elevated and sharp-pointed summit, and thence to watch the motions and scintillations, and occasional overcloudings of some bright distant star.

It is by his mastery of rhythm, as well as by his command of the apt word, or his capacity for making some illuminating analogy, that Landor stands supreme. If he has often the firmness of Dryden, he has also the subtle modulations of Congreve. But sometimes he let the rhythm run away with him; he committed that crime against literature of writing for writing's sake. And Landor's rhythm is so seductive that the anthologists have been led astray, so that the passages in Landor which are the most popular are not those which will receive the suffrage of the trained appreciators. Take the famous piece from 'Aesop and Rhodope':

> Laodamaeia died; Helen died; Leda, the beloved of Jupiter, went before. It is better to repose in the earth betimes than to sit up late; better, than to cling pertinaciously to what we feel crumbling under us, and to protract an inevitable fall. We may enjoy the present while we are insensible of infirmity and decay; but the present, like a note in music, is nothing but as it

appertains to what is past and what is to come. There are no
fields of amaranth on this side of the grave; there are no voices,
O Rhodope, that are not soon mute, however tuneful; there is
no name, with whatever emphasis of passionate love repeated,
of which the echo is not faint at last.

The rhythm is perfect, the melody haunting, but when the
passage has got itself by heart, as it soon does, it seems too
sweet: it is sentimental, as all purely atmospheric writing must
be. It has ceased to be prose without becoming poetry, and the
complexity of the rhythm betrays the simplicity of the thought.
The hardness of William Drummond is better: 'Dost thou
thinke thou leavest life too soon? Death is best young; things
faire and excellent are not of long endurance upon Earth.
Who liveth well liveth long. . . .' Nor is the utterance about
the present being like a note in music to Landor's own belief;
Epicurus had different sentiments. The truth is that the passage
expresses an emotion which remains unresolved into imagery,
and rhythm alone is not objective enough to take its place:
here Landor is false to his own classicism.

As regards his conception of the dialogue it is better to
cling to his own word 'conversations', since he made a necessary distinction between the two forms, the conversation
allowing of digressions, which 'are not unreasonable in such
discussions, and lay in a good store of humour for them'. The
dangers are of anecdote, or of becoming too dramatic, but
there is no reason why the movement of the dialogue should
be that of the mind alone. As he remarked in his conversation with Hare, 'nor is conversation a treatise', while a dialogue
should be. Not that he was always certain of his form: he
deliberately experimented. On one occasion at least he burst
into blank verse, which shows a certain hesitancy in diction;
but it is for profounder questions of form that he repays
study. The conversations with Southey are strictly dialogues;
others are really conversations. That between Duc de Richelieu
and others approaches the novel form, while the letter form of

'Pericles and Aspasia', which contains most of the essential Landor, is an interesting as well as delightful experiment. Nor was he always sure as to the object of the form he called 'conversation'. In a note to 'Ines de Castro' he remarked that 'character is the business of the dialogue'; this is not so, and his truer utterance is one of his own in the conversation with the Florentine and the English visitor: 'Principles and ideas are my objects; they must be reflected from high and low; but they must also be exhibited where people can see them best, and are most inclined to look at them.' And certainly, even in his critical conversations, though where he is indulging in line-by-line dissection, he is always aiming at 'principles and ideas'. Whether he is praising Milton or pulling Wordsworth to pieces, there is always a broad system underlying his support or his attack, and however detailed he may be he never loses sight of the object:

> In what volume of periodical criticism [Porson says], do you not find it stated that, the aim of an author being such and such, the only question is whether he has attained it? Now, instead of this being the only question to be solved, it is pretty nearly the least worthy of attention. We are not to consider whether a foolish man has succeeded in a foolish undertaking: we are to consider whether his production is worth anything, and why it is, or why it is not.

Or again:

> Poetry, like wine, requires a gentle and regular and long fermentation. What is it if it can buoy up no wisdom, no reflection; if we can throw into it none of our experience; if no repository is to be found in it for the gems we have collected, at the price sometimes of our fortunes, of our health, and of our peace?

If we cannot be impressed by his personal presence in the way his contemporaries were, so as to refer to him, like Swinburne, as 'the old demi-god with the head and heart of a lion', we cannot but be moved and stimulated by converse with the erratic, explosive, prejudiced, laughing and tender writer, who appears so solidly in his works. To most readers at any rate, he is more than a little like Boythorn in 'Bleak House' though that again is a subject forbidden by authority. They are not surprised to hear him described as being 'like an old soldier, his stalwart chest squared . . . his face lighted by a smile of so much sweetness and tenderness . . . incapable of anything on a limited scale'. His life, though it had periods of calm, was continually disrupted by fierce quarrels, with violences, misunderstandings, and vituperations, often in Latin, and sometimes coarse, the whole redeemed by an almost fabulous generosity, and an utter contempt for wealth. Beginning with an ample fortune, he was left, between the ages of eighty and ninety, with nothing to support him, and it was only owing to Browning's good offices that his family, to whom he had given everything, was induced to make him an allowance.

Any injustice or tyranny roused him to fury, and it might be said of him what he said of Blake: 'Never did a braver or better man carry the sword of justice.' Keeping aloof as he did from the pettinesses of literary life, he was always ready to praise his contemporaries. Nothing in the history of letters is finer than his criticism of Byron, who had sneered unforgivably at him, more clear-cut than the distinction he made between what is valuable and what is not in Byron's work. He saw the greatness of Shelley and Keats long before either poet was generally recognized; he was glad to call Swinburne friend. Like all able men, he was conscious of his own worth: 'What I write is not written on slate; and no finger, not of Time himself, who dips it in the cloud of years, can efface it.'

> I have since written what no tide
> Shall ever wash away, what men
> Unborn shall read o'er ocean wide
> And find Ianthe's name again.

If these and other utterances sound arrogant, it is that, as Mr. Aldington has said in a phrase itself Landorian: 'He lived so familiarly with great men, that proud speech came naturally to him.' It may readily be forgiven him, even if, as Mr. Welby says, 'Landor is not the reading of ignorant, indolent, unsensitive persons.' It may be a 'graciously austere entertainment', but Sidney Colvin was right: 'Not to know what is to be known of so remarkable a man is to be a loser. Not to be familiar with the works of so noble a writer is to be much more of a loser still.'

ROBERT SMITH SURTEES*

The Novels

SPEAKER: 'Oh, ye barber's apprentice! Oh, ye draper's assistant! Oh, ye unmitigated Mahomedon! . . . Oh you
sanctified, putrefied, perpendicular, gingerbread-
booted, counter-skippin' snob, you think because
I'm a lord and can't swear or use coarse language,
that you may do what you like.'

DOBRÉE: That was Lord Scamperdale roaring out in his usual
tones as master and owner of the flat-hat hounds,
his victim that shrewd horse-coper but good
sportsman Mr. Soapey Sponge. It is a typical bit of
Surtees, who himself gifted as so many Victorians
were with what Dr. Johnson would call 'volubility
of syllables' gives us a good many characters who
suffered, in his own words, from 'a determination
of words to the mouth'. And that, of course, is part
of the fun of Surtees: you revel in the words themselves, which he can use with refreshing originality
and unexpectedness. He is always keeping you alert
with a vivid phrase which makes you see things
with the living eye. Take, for example, in *Mr.
Romford's Hounds* his description of the snobbish
Atkinses going round the countryside calling, how
day after day they—

* Originally given as a broadcast from Leeds some time in 1952.

SPEAKER: 'Paced the weary turnpike roads, the pompous grey horses propounding their magnanimous legs with the true airing action.'

DOBRÉE: Aren't both verb and adjective glorious finds? If Surtees was a good farmer, a conscientious landlord, a militiaman, a magistrate, a Deputy Lord Lieutenant, there were two things that he really loved—hunting and writing.

SPEAKER: 'Writing, we imagine, is something like snuffing or smoking—men get into the way of it, and can't well leave it off. . . . We are never really high and dry for want of a companion so long as we can get pen, ink and paper.'

DOBRÉE: So this obviously rather lonely man filled in his solitary hours by peopling his world with a multitude of characters, drawn mainly from the hunting field, queer, but immensely lively grotesques, which are yet recognizable. Mr. Siegfried Sassoon has told us, in describing the Ringwell Hunt, that 'a large proportion of the Ringwell subscribers might have stepped straight out of his pages'. Yes and no, because he exaggerated, distorted, re-created; he is, in a sense, the Hogarth of the hunting field. Leech, admirable as he is, doesn't really do him justice. There is a *vis comica* about the world he created out of the rapscallions, the pretenders, the cheats and the snobs which takes it right out of the region of the merely ridiculous. He is in the great tradition of English comedy, devising humours like Ben Jonson, making them fantastic after the manner of Smollett, and his characters have enough life in them to allow them to exist out of their own realm. It's absurd to say, as even such enlightened people as the B.B.C. Critics on the Air said when reviewing Mr. Leonard Cooper's excellent little biography, that he's only of interest to hunting people. You might as well say that you can enjoy Sarah Gamp and Betsy Prig only if you dote on mid-wifery. Thackeray, who was not a hunting man, saw what he was after, as we can tell from a letter he wrote to Surtees.

SPEAKER: 'This is not to thank you for the grouse, but for the two last numbers of Soapey Sponge, they are capital, and the Flat Hats delightful; those fellows in spectacles divine; and Scamperdale's character perfectly odious and admirable.'

DOBRÉE: 'Odious and admirable'; that's true of most of his characters, though not all of them. For Surtees was much of a satirist; there was a purpose in a good deal of his writing. At least he tried to make out that there was, though one suspects that he gave life to his figures from the sheer delight he found in doing so, and the fun he found in the shrewd summing-up of people. He seems to have been accused of dwelling too much on the scoundrelly side of things, for he was evidently on the defensive when he stated in the preface to *Mr. Sponge's Sporting Tour*, that he was happy to be able to explain why he made—

SPEAKER: 'such a characterless character as Mr. Sponge the hero of his tale: the author will be glad if it serves to put the rising generation on their guard against specious, promiscuous acquaintance, and trains them on to the noble sport of hunting, to the ex-clusion of its mercenary, illegitimate off-shoots.'

DOBRÉE: But Sponge is delicious, the Sponge who wanted to be a gentleman but didn't quite know how. And he comes alive the moment you meet him, on page one 'mizzling along Oxford Street', having got there through 'some of those ambiguous and

tortuous streets that, appearing to lead all ways at
once, land the explorer sooner or later, on the
South side of Oxford Street, along which he goes at
'a squarrey, in-kneed, duck-toed sort of pace, regu-
lated by the bonnets, the vehicles, and the eques-
trians he met to criticize'. And bit by bit his
character emerges, especially that side of him which
is going to form the thread of the story, namely of
his fiendish skill in getting into people's houses,
only equalled by the appalling difficulty of getting
him out again. I want to dwell a little on the opening
of this book, since it gives some idea of Surtees's
real skill as a novelist; and then we see the setting
from which Sponge starts, to return to again at the
end, the busy, confused London of early Victorian
times. It is a fascinatingly live pen-picture: but
before it is read, I would remind you that Surtees
used the word 'cad' in the same sense as Dickens and
Thackeray did, namely to mean a 'bus conductor:
here, then, is Sponge, at the corner of the Edgware
Road, catching a 'bus to the country.

SPEAKER: 'Behold him now at the Edgware Road end, eyeing
the 'buses with a wanting-a-ride like air, instead of
the contemptuous sneer he generally adopts towards those uncouth productions. Red, green, blue,
drab, cinnamon-colour, passed and crossed, and
jostled, and stopped, and blocked, and the cads
telegraphed, and winked, and nodded, and smiled,
and slanged, but Mr. Sponge regarded them
not. . . .

'Mark him as he stands at the corner. He sees
what he wants, it's the chequered one with the red
and blue wheels that the Bayswater ones have got
between them, and that the St. John's Wood and
two Western Railway ones are trying to get into

trouble by crossing. What a row! How the ruffians whip, and stamp, and storm and all but pick each other's horses' teeth with their poles, how the cads gesticulate, and the passengers imprecate! now the bonnets are out of the windows, and the row increases. Six coachmen cutting and storming, six cads sawing the air, sixteen ladies in flowers screaming, six-and-twenty sturdy passengers swearing they will 'fine then all', and Mr. Sponge is the only cool person in the scene.'

DOBRÉE: Surtees always puts his people in their setting; but if there is no excuse for not seeing them in action, there is still less for not knowing exactly what they looked like, or what they wore. And what he enormously enjoys is the description of some idiosyncracy, such as that of Sponge's very shady horse-coping confederate, Mr. Benjamin Buckram, who would gather in his hand the silver he had in his breeches' pocket, and let the coins fall one by one to punctuate his remarks, or, by way of a paragraph, so to speak, would let a regular avalanche of silver slide down. So a deal of the best in Surtees comes from keen, detailed, delighted observation, though a good deal also from sheer comic inventiveness. There is, for instance, Jack Spraggon, who was Lord Scamperdale's double, down to the black-rimmed spectacles they could share between them, and whom Scamperdale employed to do his swearing for him; but best of all, perhaps, is Mr. Boyston, the friend of Mr. Jovey Jessop, whose life entailed a great deal of wet conviviality, but who was forbidden by his doctor to drink. So Boyston always accompanied Jovey Jessop as his Jug, into which was poured all the liquor Jessop wasn't allowed to swallow. The Jug, as he was always called, occupies rather a large place in the book, which is *Plain or Ringlets?*, in which there is not much about hunting, but which is full of the bustle of picnics and dinners, of match-making and the judging of reputations, with Admiration Jack, the Duke of Tergiversation, old 'sivin and four's elivin' the banker, and Mr. and Mrs. Bouderkins, the social climbers. It all rattles along with enormous gusto, and you enjoy the rather obvious social satire because Surtees so whole-heartedly enjoys depicting his fools, and here must have chuckled immensely over his ironical endings.

But let us look at some of the books which more copiously illustrate Surtees' best performances—his descriptions of rooted country types, for instance. Take Mr. Lonnergan in *Mr. Romford's Hounds*. He was known as Lord Lonnergan because he had been the previous Lord Lovetin's agent, 'and had hardly been able to realize the fact the he (Lonnergan) was not the real owner of the property, and the present Viscount an intruder'.

SPEAKER: 'Lord Lonnergan was one of a now nearly bygone generation, whose antiquity is proclaimed by their dress. He wore a large puffy shirt-frill and a puddingey white tie with flowing ends, a step collared buff vest, and a blue coat with bright buttons. He had long adhered to tights and Hessians, and it was only when he found himself alone in his glory that he put his fat legs into trousers. He was a porcupine-headed little man, who tied his cravat so tight as to look as if he was going to throttle himself. He was a short, sallow, plethoric, wheezy, scanty-whiskered man, with eyes set very high up in his head, like garret windows: a long unmeaning-looking face, surmounted with a nose like a pear. His mouth was

M

significant of nothing except an aptitude for eating . . . he had a voluminous double chin.

'He drew his great warming-pan-like watch
from his fob with a massive kitchen jack-like gold
chain . . .'

DOBRÉE: . . . and so on, while his actions go with what he
looks like. Most unforgettable of all perhaps are Mr.
and Mrs. Jogglebury Crowdey upon whom Soapey
sponged for so long that the poor man decided to
sell up his property and emigrate. Soapey had been
invited because Mrs. Jogglebury hoped to settle her
numerous brood by providing rich god-parents for
them, and Mr. Sponge *seemed* the very thing. Fat,
wheezy, bellows-to-mend Jogglebury himself was
going to enrich them by his collection of what he
called 'gibbey-sticks', an horrific accumulation of
walking sticks which he had cut out of hedge-rows
and copses and plantations with heads which he
carved into portraits of monarchs or great men,
series after series of King Williams, of Byrons,
Napoleons, Disraelis, of beasts and birds and fishes.

SPEAKER: 'He had accumulated a vast quantity—thousands;
the garret at the top of his house was quite full, so
were most of the closets, while the rafters in the
kitchen, and cellars, and out-houses, were crowded
with others in a state of *déshabille*. He calculated his
stock at immense worth, we don't know how many
thousands of pounds; and as he cut, and puffed, and
wheezed, and modelled, he chuckled, and thought
how well he was providing for his family'.

DOBRÉE: Surely one of the strangest grotesques in literature.
The whole episode, with his conversations with his
wife, the coaching of the putative god-child, the
efforts to dislodge Soapey, is one of the most diverting bits of brisk comedy in any of our novels.

But if Surtees' main object in writing—apart from the pleasure it gave him—was to give easy reading to a vast mass of semi-literates who might be got to read something a little more nourishing than the local newspaper or Mogg's Cab Fares, he had several very definite things to say. First of all he wanted to give a loose to his prejudices—as for instance the Duke of Tergiversation, Lord Lovetin and others. Lord Scamperdale was to some extent redeemed by his love of hunting, but was otherwise odious; and there was Lord Reynard, of whom his ex-huntsman wrote to his successor:

SPEAKER: 'I hope you old man keeps a cleaner tongue in his head than he did when I was premier. I always say there was a good bargeman lost when they made him a lord'.

DOBRÉE: As an officer in the militia he had a hearty hatred of regular soldiers, and flinched from the sight of them in the hunting-field. His greatest creation, Jorrocks, shared his opinion.

SPEAKER: 'The top-sawyers of the 'unt will be close on the 'untsman. There will not be many of these; but should there be a barrack in the neighbourhood, some soger officers will most likely mex up and ride at the 'ardest rider among 'em. The dragon soger officer is the most dangerous, and may be known by the viskers under his nose.'

DOBRÉE: What he hated with a deep bone-hatred was any kind of pretentiousness. He was essentially a country squire, happy in looking after his small estate in Co. Durham, very solicitous for the welfare of the land, an authority on good farming. He was a country conservative of the good type, and as such despised all upstarts, all snobs, as he called them, using the word in the same sense as his friend

Thackeray, as denoting those who meanly aspire after mean things—being thought better than you really were, pretending to be richer than you really were. He liked the modest, the people who thought less of themselves than of the job they were doing. He had no manner of use for men who went out hunting to show off, who rode for riding's sake and not to see hounds. He loved hunting as a scientific sport, and not as a flashy competitive amusement. He had nothing but scorn for the pretender, the humbug, the charlatan, the scraper. His satirical itch accounts for there being so few lovable people among his characters. But he was also a shrewd observer of what was happening in the country, especially of the changes the railways were bringing about. If they did harm by bringing plenty of riff-raff into the country, so that local race-meetings became the happy hunting ground of cheats and scoundrels and welshing bookies (what he thought about racing he put into the mouth of the lawyer Ballivant in *Plain or Ringlets?*), he saw how they were enormously civilizing the little country squire, the hawbuck, and how the clubs in London were helping the progress. People who read novels as social historians won't waste their time if they read Surtees, not only the great novels, but *Ask Mamma*, *Hawbuck Grange*, and especially *Hillingdon Hall*, though perhaps that, as a novel, is the least successful of his works. That he was a reading man is clear from his frequent quotations from, or allusions to, works of literature. How wise he was you can tell from the aphorisms scattered through his books. 'Take not out your 'ounds on a werry windy day' doesn't apply only to hunting, nor was it meant to. Nor was 'What a huntsman I'd be if it weren't for the leaps.' He had a great sense of how human beings should treat each other—and all this is presented in terms which reveal the literary man: the born writer is betrayed by the zest with which he writes.

His great triumph, it is agreed, is *Handley Cross*, where he deals not only with hunting, but with what he was almost as fond of portraying, the life of a popular watering place. It is a densely populated region he asks us to live in for a while, with Miserrimus Doleful, the Master of the Ceremonies, with the A.D.C. who was showered with invitations till it was discovered that the initials stood for Assistant Drains Commissioner; with the little old man with the thundering good library who when put out at breakfast threw his cup through the window and clapped the saucer on his head (a George Borrow touch that), Mrs. Muleygrubs and the ladies known as 'the Crusher' and 'the Bloomer', the good farmers, the bad farmers, the horse-copers, Pomponius Ego (in real life the great Apperley who wrote under the name of 'Nimrod'), and dozens of other important figures or smaller fry, all living a life of tremendous activity. But in the centre of all, naturally, is the great M.F.H. himself, John Jorrocks, the successful grocer from Great Coram Street in London, and the people around him—his abrupt wife, his charming niece Belinda, who is the only attractive female character, in contrast with the famous Lucy Glitters, late of the London theatres and such a first-class whipper-in, who exacts only admiration.

Not to know James Pigg is like not knowing Sam Weller; no doubt they wander together about the Elysian Fields, 'hand in hand, like the sign of the

Mutual Insurance Hoffice' as the M.F.H. would
say, the one being witty and wise in cockney, the
other retorting in dialect of the Cannynewcassel he
came from. Long, lanky, spindle-shanked, with
flowing grey-streaked locks, a weather-beaten face
lighted up by hazel eyes, and tobacco juice always
simmering down the deep furrows of his chin, he is
the admirable simpleton, devoted only to hounds
and hunting, though he can't refuse a glass of
brandy. Then there is Benjamin, 'a stunted, pasty-
faced, white-headed ginnified boy, that might be
any age from eight to eighteen, and as idle and mis-
chievous a brat as it was possible to conceive, sharp
as a needle, and quick as lightning'—addicted to
marmalade and overmatching his master. And
Charley Stobbs, Surtees' only decent and likable
young man, who pursued the fox and Belinda at
the same time. Greatest of all, Jorrocks himself,
fat, uncouth, greedy, but who redeems all by his
whole-hearted passion for the chase. There is a good
deal of Surtees himself in Jorrocks, one feels, the
same hatred of pretension, though he knew 'when
to butter a booby and when to snub a snob'. He had
read a good deal, and, like Surtees, could quote the
poets, mainly Somerville's *The Chace:* it was Somerville who described hunting as 'the sport of kings
and the image of war without its guilt', the shrewd
tea-merchant adding 'and only twenty-five per cent
of the danger'. When he lost a fox, he could even
quote from Addison's *Cato,* 'It's not in mortals to
command success'; and if he might pain the classicist
by describing Pigg as a *lusus naturae* or a loose 'un
by nature—and other quasi-latinisms as outrageous, vy, dash my vig, as he'd say, what does
that matter? But let us see him and Pigg in action on

the famous Cat and Custard-Pot day. Jorrocks and
Stobbs were late for the meet, having been delayed
over a horse; and, sad to say, the field had made Pigg
drunk on brandy before the Master arrived. After
an exchange of amenities, Jorrocks dismisses Pigg,
and starts to take the hounds home; but then, on
the way—

SPEAKER: 'a sudden something shot through the body of the
late, loitering, indifferent hounds, apparently in-
fluencing them with a sort of invisible agency.
Another instant, and a wild snatch or two right and
left ended in a whisper and a general shoot up the
lane. "A fox! for a 'underd" muttered our Master,
drawing breath as he eyed them. "A fox! for two-
and-twenty 'underd!" continued he, as Priestess
feathered but spoke not. "A fox! for a million!"
roared he, as old Ravager threw his tongue lightly
but confidently, and Jorrocks cheered him to the
echo. "A fox! for 'alf the national debt". . . .
Jorrocks, cocking his cap on his ear seats himself
plump in his great saddle, and, gathering his reins,
gallops after them in the full grin of delight. . . .
The pace mended as they went, and Jorrocks hugged
himself with the idea of killing a fox without
Pigg. . . . He began to bet himself hats that they'd
kill him, and went vowing that he'd offer to Diana
if he did. . . . Crash! now go the hounds upon an
old thorn-fence, stuck on a low sod-bank, making
Jorrocks shudder at the sound'.

DOBRÉE: Over goes Stobbs, without doing anything for his
followers.

SPEAKER: 'Go on, Binjimin! go on! Now,' cries Jorrocks,
cantering up, cracking his whip, as if he wanted to
take it in his stride, but in reality to frighten Ben
over to break it. 'Go on, ye miserable man-monkey

of a boy!' as Xerxes now turned tail, nearly up-
setting our master—'Oh you epitome of a tailor!'
groaned Jorrocks; 'you're of no more use wi'
'ounds than a lady's maid,—do believe I could make
as good a wipper-in out of a carrot! See! you've set
my quad a-refusin', and I'll bet a guinea 'at to a
half-crown wide-awake he'll not face another fence
today. Come hup, I say, you ugly beast!' now
roared Jorrocks, pretending to put Arterxerxes at
it, but in reality holding him hard by the head.—
'Get off! ye useless apology of a hosier and pull it
down, or I'll give you such a wopping as'll send
you to Blair Athol for the rest of the day.'

DOBRÉE: They get off again, and Jorrocks catches up with
the hounds; but soon the line is foiled by a flock
of sheep, and Charley Stobbs fails to pick it up
again.

SPEAKER: ' "Humph," grunted our master, reviewing his
cast, "the ship must ha' heat 'im, or he's wanished
into this hair;" adding, "jest put 'em on to me
Charley, whilst I makes one o' Mr. Craven Smith's
patent all-round-my-'at casts, for that beggar
Binjimin's of no more use with a pack of 'ounds than
a hopera box would be to a cow, or a frilled shirt to
a pig." '

DOBRÉE: Even that, however, is no good, and the hounds
throw up.

SPEAKER: ' "Well, it's nine 'underd and fifty thousand petties,"
muttered our master now that the last of the
stoopers had got up their heads, "it's nine 'underd
and fifty thousand petties that I hadn't got close
away at his brush, for I'd ha' killed 'im to a dead
certainty. Never was a fox better 'unted than that!
Science, patience, judgment, skill, everything that
constitutes an 'untsman—Goodhall, himself, couldn't

ha' done it better! But it's not for mortals to command success", sighed our now greatly dejected master. . . . But just as Mr. Jorrocks was reigning in his horse to blow his hounds together, a wild, shrill, view holloo, just such as one as a screech-owl gives on a clear frosty night, sounded through the country, drawing all eyes to Camperdown Hill, where against a blue sky sat a Wellington-statue-like equestrian with his cap in the air, waving and shouting for hard life.

'The late lethargic hounds pricked up their ears, and before Mr. Jorrocks could ejaculate the word "Pigg!" the now excited pack had broke away, and were streaming full cry across country to where Pigg was perched.'

DOBRÉE: So the hunt is up once more, the pace getting fast and furious, and Mr. Jorrocks gets off the exhausted Arterxerxes to change to the Xerxes Ben had ridden more like a second horse than that of a whip. So Jorrocks is off again, all elbows and legs.

SPEAKER: ' "By 'eavens, it's sublime!" exclaimed he, eyeing the hounds streaming away over a hundred-acre pasture below. "By 'eavens, it's sublime! 'ow they go, screechin' and towlin' along, jest like a pocketfull o' marbles. 'Ow the old wood re-echoes their melody, and the old castle seemingly takes pleasure to repeat the sound. A Julienn concert's nothin' to it. No, not all the bands in the country put together."

' "How I wish I was a heagle!" now exclaimed Mr. Jorrocks, eyeing the wide-stretching vale before him. "How I wish I was a heagle 'overin' over 'em, seein' which 'ound has the scent, which hasn't, and which are runnin' frantic for blood."

' "To guide a scent well over a country for a length of time, through all the changes and chances o' the chase, and among all the difficulties usually encountered, requires the best and most experienced abilities," added he, shortening his hold of his horse, as he now puts his head down the steep part of the hill. Away Jorrocks went, wobbling like a great shape of red Noyau jelly.'

DOBRÉE: The whole thing ends with a kill, and a sentimental reconciliation with Pigg, sentimental at least as far as Jorrocks is concerned.

Those extracts from the two chapters of the Cat and Custard Pot day may give some faint flavour of this great comic creation: but apart from that, it is worth while to live for a little in the ebullient Surtees world. Once read, the figures recur to the mind's memory. An extraordinary phantasmagoria of marionettes and more than marionettes passes across one's vision, of people and scenes of hints and hunt balls, there are whispers in one's ears of conversations in stables and streets, in boudoirs and banqueting halls, at the covert side and in railway pubs. And even if the words do not linger, the figures stand out in the general bustle. One would recognize them anywhere by their looks alone—for who would fail to greet Sir Harry Scattercash with his strings all flying? Or by their gestures? Cannot you hear Mr. Benjamin Buckram letting his coins slide down his pocket?

But perhaps it's detached scenes or gestures that we see, phrases that we hear. Mr. Jorrocks dashes his vig and dances with glee about the fox's corpse; or he is floundering through Pinch-me-near Forest, that 'incorrigible mountain', that 'unpardonable forest' as he called it; or drowning in the swimming-bath at Ongar Park: Soapey Sponge cannons into Lord Scamperdale, who, swearing that he cannot swear, swears on: Facey Romford gets his hounds round him with the help of his pretended sister, Mrs. Sponge, the late Lucy Glitters; Mr. Jogglebury Crowdey wheezes where his verbs ought to be; Boyston acts as Jug to Jovey Jessop; Binjimin sticks his fingers into the marmeylad; old 'Sivin-and four's-ilivin' counts his bills, Jorrocks' peacock, Gabriel Junks, prophesies the weather; Mr. Jorrocks in the ecstacy of his fox-hunting dreams kicks his wife out of bed; and over them all hovers the airy spirit of James Pigg, invoking Cannynewcassel, and keeping the tambourine a'rowlin' while he offers you a gob of tobacco.

WILLIAM MAKEPEACE
THACKERAY*

'THERE is a man in our own days,' Charlotte Brontë wrote
in her dedication to Thackeray of the second edition of
Jane Eyre, 'whose words are not framed to tickle delicate
ears; who, to my thinking, comes before the great ones of
society, much as the son of Imlah came before the throned
Kings of Judah and Israel; and who speaks a truth as deep. . . .
I regard him as the first social regenerator of the day.'

Thackeray was somewhat taken aback. 'It quite flustered
and upset me,' he wrote: 'Is it true, I wonder?' He might well
ask himself if he was really 'the very master of that working
corps who would restore to rectitude the warped system of
things'. Certainly there was a moral in each of his books; indeed he insisted all through on two or three morals, but he
was no fiery prophet. This man of the world it is true, was not
altogether genial, and a certain Yates in the gossip column of
'Town Talk' (Vol. IV. 89) could say of him:

> his bearing is cold and uninviting, his style of conversation
> either openly cynical, or affectionately good-natured; his
> *bonhomie* (sic) is forced, his wit biting, his pride easily touched. . . .

He may not always have been genial—who is?—but this man
of the world was essentially 'pacable', to use a favourite word
of his. So we need not be surprised to find Trollope in his
Thackeray saying that he was:

* Rewritten from two earlier essays on Thackeray.

. . . one of the most soft-hearted of human beings, sweet as Charity itself, who went about the world dropping pearls, doing good and never wilfully inflicting a wound.

He was, however, clear-eyed above everything, and refused to take people at their own, or for that matter, the world's valuation: he despised snobbery and pretentiousness, and believed firmly in what Keats called 'the holiness of the heart's affections'.

The fact would seem to be that his voice was discordant with that of his age. For the Victorians, however much we may respect them, as we now do (the pendulum is perhaps swinging a little too far from the derisive contempt of a generation ago), did, we feel, too much like to look at the rosy side of things—at least where the average middle-class person was concerned. You could reveal 'the tradition of the people', after the manner of Kingsley and Mrs. Gaskell, or even of Dickens, if you were either evangelistic or pitiful enough, but not the moral condition of the ruling classes. How otherwise could Trollope, again, have written in a rather happy redressing of the balance in favour of the Thackeray family: 'Miss Broughton's novels are not so sweet-savoured as those of Miss Thackeray, and are, therefore, less true to nature.' It is clear, however, that there was something about Thackeray which annoyed his contemporaries, just as there is something which annoys people now. Yet it would be difficult for anyone to read his letters and not at least relent: many will feel warmly towards the man whatever they think of the author.

At all events he enjoyed life as a fascinating spectacle; he liked to have his glass of sherry and his talk at the Garrick ('a man's first glass of wine in the day is a great event'); he understood and enormously sympathized with the ardours and peccadilloes of the young, and it irked him that he could not write about them: 'Since the author of Tom Jones was buried, no writer of fiction among us has been permitted to depict to his utmost power a MAN', he complained in the Preface to

Pendennis: Victorian prudery hampered this solid, sensitive eighteenth-century man. 'If truth is not always pleasant', he said bluntly, 'at any rate truth is best.' He told enough of it ironically to prick the optimistic bubble of the Victorians, who tried to shove off his strokes with 'Pooh! Cynicism!' Thackeray heard enough of this charge. In a letter of 1857 he wrote:

> knowing very well the common cry against me that I am mis-anthropical, bitter, and so forth, whereas, please God, my heart is full of anything but unkindness towards the people who believe me such a cynic. No human brain is big enough to grasp the whole truth—and mine can take in no doubt but a very infinitesimal portion of it; but truth such as I know I must tell, and go on telling while my lungs last.

Was Charlotte Brontë so far out after all?

We may look at his life for a moment, as giving us a clue to many of his themes. He was born in Calcutta, where, four years later his father died. When six years old he was sent to England, and shortly afterwards his mother married Captain Carmichael-Smyth. In due course he went to the Charterhouse school—whence its appearance in so many of his novels—and then to Trinity College, Cambridge, which he left without taking his degree, having gambled away £1,500. After some indeterminate years, as an art student in Paris, eating dinners at the Middle Temple—we hear about art in *The Newcomes* and elsewhere, and about the Temple in *Pendennis*—in 1833 he lost the bulk of his money in the failure of an Indian bank, as Colonel Newcome was to do. He was helped in this crisis by his maternal grandmother, the original of old Miss Crawley in *Vanity Fair*, and by his cousin Mary Graham, who was imi-tated as Laura in *Pendennis*.

He finally settled down to journalism and novel-writing, in 1835 marrying Miss Shawe. They had two daughters, one of whom was to become Lady Ritchie (Anne Thackeray, the novelist), the other Mrs. Leslie Stephen: but in 1840 his wife became insane, and had to be detained in an asylum for the most part of her life. A few years later, Mrs. Brookfield, the wife of a fashionable preacher who is close cousin to Charles Honeyman in *The Newcomes*, became the emotional centre of his life, except for his children, to whom he was devoted, and for whom he worked enormously hard for the rest of his not very long career. Besides writing novels, the great six and the minor ones, he laboured at producing sketches, verse, travel letters, criticism, and, he moaned 'Punch, Punch, Punch!' where his *Book of Snobs* appeared. He also undertook lecture tours, both in England and in America, where he got much of his material for *The Virginians;* but he hated the 'mountebank performance' even when talking about subjects that he liked, such as *The Four Georges*, or *English Humourists*. However, it paid, and he rejoiced in the fattening roll of dollars that would make his wife's maintenance secure, and provide a patrimony for his daughters. So he came through, and thought of going back to painting, or sitting for Parliament: but before he could release himself, he died, on Christmas Eve 1863.

Readers of Thackeray will find that his life will account for most of his themes and scenes: he wrote, as he tells us, of what he knew about—inventing, exaggerating, constructing, of course, so that, as his Mr. Batchelor said in *Lovel the Widower*, 'though it is all true, there is not a word of truth in it'. We see the reason, then, for the constantly recurring themes of gambling, art, the seamy side of life such as a law-student might learn of—blackmail occurs in *Pendennis* and *Philip*—a good deal of tavern life, and above all for the upper-middle-class social existence in which he himself was plunged, and observed both warmly and sardonically. Yet there is one theme which will appear to come from outside Thackeray's own experience —namely the lifelong hopeless devotion of a man faithful to his first love, as with Henry Esmond, Colonel Newcome, Dobbin in *Vanity Fair* (a character based on Archdeacon Allen); it is made fun of a little in the case of Mr. Batchelor. Allied to this is the theme of the marriage-market, against which Thackeray inveighs at inordinate length, and, it must be confessed, with infuriating reiteration. These themes have their origin in the life of his mother. As a young girl she fell in love with a gallant but impecunious officer in the Bengal Engineers; her parents forbade the marriage, locked her up, and vainly tried to extort from her a promise to give up Ensign Carmichael-Smyth. After a short while she was told that he had died of a sudden fever. Sent to some cousins in India, she there contracted a sufficiently opulent and brilliant marriage with Richmond Thackeray, with whom she was happy enough. Then one day he announed that he had invited a charming new acquaintance to dinner, an Engineer officer: he came, and to Mrs. Thackeray's agonized astonishment, he turned out to be Carmichael-Smyth. All parties seem to have behaved admirably; but soon after the death of Richmond Thackeray, the novelist's mother married her first love. The implications of all this haunted Thackeray throughout his life, whence the frequent appearance of the two connected themes.

It is often said that a writer reveals himself as artist more clearly in his letters than in his creative work. This would seem to depend a good deal upon the writer. Keats, Tchekov, and Fournier could write miraculously revealing letters about their art, but we do not learn very much from the correspondence of Racine and Boileau. For art is possibly a specialized function of the personality; a man may show his wholeness, his real stature, only when warmed by the heat of creation. At other times something of him lies dormant, or at least imperfectly expressed.

Thackeray seldom talks about his art in his letters, which are very amusing, though he does about his work, as work. It would seem that the thoughts that moved him attained ripeness only when he was in the full flush of creative activity. His letters are oddly unfulfilled even when he is talking to intimate friends. We get an illustration of this in Mr. Gordon Ray's admirable edition: on 18th December, 1848, he writes to Mrs. Brookfield:

> we will love each other while we may here and afterwards, if you go first you will kneel for me in heaven and bring me there —if I, I swear the best thought I have is to remember that I shall have your love surviving me and with a constant tenderness blessing my memory. I can't all perish living in your heart . . . if I were to die to-morrow I think I should leave two women behind me in whose hearts the tenderest remembrance of me wd. live as thank God it deserves to do.

In the chapter in *The History of Henry Esmond* headed 'The 29th December', we read:

> Gracious God, who was he, weak and friendless creature, that such a love should be poured out upon him? Not in vain— not in vain has he lived,—hard and thankless should he be to think so—that has such a treasure given him. What is ambition compared to that? but selfish vanity. To be rich, to be famous? What do these profit a year hence, when other names sound louder than yours, when you lie hidden away under ground, along with the idle titles engraven on your coffin? But only true love lives after you,—follows your memory with secret blessing,—or precedes you, and intercedes with you. *Non omnis moriar*,—if dying, I yet live in a tender heart or two; nor am I lost and hopeless living, if a sainted departed soul still loves and prays for me.

Such matters, naturally, are only of secondary interest to the reader of the novels. There are three things he will ask. 'Are the stories in themselves holding, interesting, exciting? Can I understand, sympathize with, love or hate the characters? Am I let into a world which confirms and enlarges my experience?' The stories are in themselves enthralling, and sometimes an atmosphere of gripping excitement is created. Will Beatrice Esmond marry the Pretender? Of course we know beforehand that she will not, yet as we read *Esmond* we shelve our historical knowledge, and feel that the climax of the

N

novel, swift as it is, does not go half fast enough. What will be
the end of Becky Sharp? we wonder as we read *Vanity Fair*, and
of the preposterous Jos? And will Dobbin marry Amelia? In
Pendennis we become desperately anxious as to whether the cat
will be let out of the bag as regards the Clavering family. And
how actual and vivid the characters are! Who would not
recognize, who has not met, though with the idiosyncracies that
make an individual rather than a type, Clive Newcome, say,
the Warringtons, the amiable Lady Clavering, or the lesser
Crawleys? We know exactly what they all look like. And they
are subtler than is usually supposed, not all black or all white,
as one hears it said they are.

Take even that paragon of simple virtue, Colonel Newcome, whose obstinate folly nearly brought disaster on the son
for whom he lived: and the other side of the medal, figuring old
Lady Kew and Major Pendennis, whose snobbery—the mean
aspiring after mean things—itself involved sacrifices and
efforts demanding stern qualities of character; and in the end
we come rather to love and respect the old Major, as Thackeray
seems to have done, so staunch he was in his triviality. There
are, to be sure, the very black, such as Becky Sharp, Altamont,
and Dr. Firmin, as there are the shining white, such as Laura
Pendennis, 'the little sister', Warrington of the Upper Temple,
and old Bows: we meet of course dozens of contemptible
worldlings, the Twysdens, shall we say, and the lovable
rapscallions of the 'Captain' Costigan breed, drawn with the
skill of the born comic writer and natural caricaturist; and
these are mixed with the normal neither good nor bad but very
much alive human beings that most of his heroes are.

Thackeray abundantly created a world, active, vociferous,
buzzing with all sorts and conditions of men and women,
loving and lovable, hideously unscrupulous, hateful or piti-
able; people whom one can admire, others fit only to be despised. It is one world; the same persons interweave through the
great novels, and even the lesser ones. People whose story be-

gan in the very early *A Shabby Genteel Story* complete their
lives in Thackeray's last finished work, *The Adventures of
Philip:* Arthur Pendennis, the novelist, writes the history of
the Newcomes and the biography of Philip Firmin; the same
minor characters, such as J. J. Ridley, the painter, appear in
several books. We can become absorbed in this thickly populated world, so glamorous and so mean, so full of high hopes
and of bitter disillusions, of attainment (but it is moral attainment), of compromises, or wreck. You may complain with the
sticklers for form that the novels are not well enough constructed; but Thackeray's was a popular method; his novels
flow along like great broad streams upon which we float in
varied company, observing a thousand things as we go, all to
the accompaniment of a prose that is effortless but marvellously musical.

As for the great scenes, the novels abound with them. Remember Rawdon Crawley rushing back from the spunging
house to his wife Becky, who had said she was ill in bed, to
find her enjoying a *tête-à-tête* supper with Lord Steyne, whose
forehead he scars for ever by throwing at it a jewel that the
rich old sinner had given his wife! Very subtle scenes sometimes, too, worthy of Henry James. Take as one instance the
scene where Ethel Newcome shows Lord Kew, who wants to
marry her, an anonymous letter vilifying him. Can one forget
his silence, their separation, and when, on seeing her again
after an hour, his holding out his hand to her, and then:

> 'My dear', he said, 'if you had loved me you would never
> have shown me that letter.' It was his only reproof. After that
> he never reproved nor advised her.
> Ethel blushed. 'You are very brave and generous, Frank,'
> she said, bending her head, 'and I am captious and wicked' . . .
> He kissed her little hand. Lady Anne, who was in the room
> when these few words passed between the two in a very low
> tone, thought it was a reconciliation.
> Ethel knew it was a renunciation on Kew's part—she never
> liked him so much as at that moment.

Or think of the tremendous scene where Dobbin so stag-
geringly tells Amelia Sedley how unworthy she is of his unswerving devotion.

And all the time, in great Hall or cheap lodging-house, in
London or Paris or Baden-Baden, Thackeray is dissecting,
analyzing, passing favourable or damning judgments on these
very ordinary if unusually vital people, piercing below the
surface of Victorian society to the motives that really animate
people, criticizing, not the social structure, but the individuals
who make up that structure—human nature, in fact. He gave
no exhibitions of heated moral fervour; the Victorians rather
enjoyed that sort of castigation, but they got from him what
they did not altogether enjoy—comic ridicule, and a deep dis-
taste served up with a dry flavouring, so much so that when he
went to America the people there were surprised to find him
so easy, lovable, and sociable.

Was he then, far from being cynical, unendurably sentimental, as the charge against him now is? Yes and no. No,
because after all he was sentimental, if you like to call it so,
about the right things; paternal and especially maternal
affection (Helen Pendennis is a portrait of his mother), the
saving grace of devoted feeling, of young love, unswerving
loyalty in masculine friendship, courage moral and physical.
Yes, because there are phrases we flinch at—Ethel's 'little'
hand perhaps—while some people, Laura Pendennis for example (in real life Mary Graham became more like the heartless
and silly Blanche Amory) are insufferably good and right and
righteous. And Amelia Sedley! Yet caution is advisable.
Thackeray himself calls Amelia insipid; she was not his ideal
woman, and Dobbin, after he had married her, found that his
daughter, and even his history of the Punjab, were more interesting. But Thackeray too often irritatingly holds up the
story for the sake of long-winded sermonising; too often
young lovers pass hours gazing at the windows behind which
they believe the beloved to be sleeping; there are too many

pages, amusing though they often are, about skeletons in cupboards.

It is often complained, therefore, that he continually steps out of his novels and preaches at you as author. Yet, as Professor Geoffrey Tillotson pointed out in his brilliant study, *Thackeray the Novelist*, it is the narrator, someone other than himself, who takes the stage. Nevertheless, today we feel that the moral should be implicit in the story, and need not be rubbed in. But then Thackeray, by this method, makes you, so to speak, a fellow-conspirator; the author is telling you a tale by the fireside, and reserves the right to break off when he wishes to discuss the issues with you, to moralize, to draw conclusions about the general behaviour of people. Not that he hoped to reform humanity; the persons in his novels do not change their characters. He believed that men and women remain much as they are born; it is only circumstances that leave their stamp on them. Thus the fascinating Beatrix Esmond, at bottom selfish, ambitious, and without much heart, could become nothing other than the astringent old Baroness Bernstein; Ethel Newcome, basically good, temporarily distorted by old Lady Kew, becomes the admirable loving wife of Clive; that eager, generous, impulsive youth Arthur Pendennis settles down as the benevolent middle-aged paterfamilias.

But what, one asks, is the final moral, the total impression of what Thackeray has to say, to give us, apart from his strictures upon the futility, the waste of energy, of Vanity Fair? Is it nothing romantic, revolutionary, or explosive; he waves us on to no Utopia, social or spiritual, towards which we must strive. He inculcates, rather, a stoical acceptance of things, in a world that we must try to make more habitable, by observing the pieties, by decent behaviour, by cherishing the Christian virtues in which this agnostic so firmly believed. But, as he packs into the last brief paragraph of *Vanity Fair*, he warns us not to expect too much:

Vanitas Vanitatum! Which of us is happy in this world? Which
of us has his desire? or, having it, is satisfied?—Come, children,
let us shut up the box and the puppets, for our play is played out.

He himself took his part with all his energies, lived his life
'excessively', it has been said; lived it so hard, enjoying so
much of it amid his griefs, that he burnt himself out pre-
maturely.

OUIDA*

IN the 'seventies, a dashing woman of about thirty-five might
have been seen driving about the neighbourhood of Florence
in an equipage of high style, usually accompanied by her
mother, and surrounded with a menagerie of animals. She was
fair, with a thin, oval face; masses of golden-brown hair over-
hung large, dark-blue eyes, while her body terminated in small
hands and feet. A charming woman; but, unfortunately, she
had 'a voice like a carving knife'. This was Maria Louise (de la)
Ramée, better known as Ouida, who, born in 1839 enjoyed a
period of resounding popularity, with its consequent wealth,
but who faded from public favour and died in poverty in
1908, barely subsisting on a Civil List pension obtained for her
only the year before.

Yes, she was enormously read, but her books were not
allowed to lie about on drawing-room tables. She was too
glamorous; she was, they said, 'unwholesome'; but then that
was part of the thrill, for she was in rebellion against rigid
Victorian conventions, current moral, religious, and domestic
ideals; and the worst of it was that, in the light of her burning
vision, these ideals did, after all, appear a little mean. If she
was 'flashy', the ideals were tawdry. No, one must not confess
to reading her, except to mock at her absurd mistakes, her
'diverting inaccuracies'—did not the critics with their fastidious taste pick ever so many holes in her? (till two of the most
fastidious, Mr. G. S. Street and Mr. Max Beerbohm, came to

* This article first appeared in *The Listener,* 10 August, 1932 and is reprinted
by kind permission of the Editor.

the rescue)—why, one could no more confess to liking her than today one can confess, except as a sign of being very, very highbrow, to liking thrillers. For thrillers was exactly what she did write; not simply physical thrillers, but moral and emotional ones, in which we abandon ourselves to moral and emotional sensation just as we do to excitement over physical thrills in the sensation novels of today; her wicked are so deeply wicked, her good so extravagantly good, the issues between them so strenuously fought out, that one abandons any hankering after analysis, probability, subtlety, and floats, even now, deliciously on the great wave of her exuberant, superabundant vitality.

The difficulty is not to account for her old popularity, but for her neglect at the present day; indeed we feel that, could Ouida arise again, she would only have to change her idiom a little, and she would catch us all once more; indeed that best-seller, Mr. P. C. Wren's *Beau Geste*, is only *Under Two Flags* written in a different language. What we really resent in Ouida today is her lavishness; lavish is the word one would choose to describe her predominant quality. Beauty is heaped on perfection, vileness is flung on the top of degradation, in a manner repugnant to our weaker digestions, and all in an immense torrent of words. But then the Victorians revelled in such spates of language, even in their best literature—think only of Carlyle and Browning—and that we do not so revel is not necessarily to our credit, for what may masquerade as restraint may really be thinness. No doubt, however, it is over-luxurious to relish such phrases as this from Ouida's *Strathmore*, written with such obvious delight in its alliteraton: 'threw his ermine over his emptiness, covered all cancans with his coronet, and hushed all whispers with his wealth'. But then this luxury, not only in words, but spread over everything, making scenery better than it ever was in real life, turning a boudoir into a paradise, and infecting souls and bodies with a super-humanity which dazzles (where it does not stun)—how refreshing! what a delicious escape! what a haven, what an orgy of what the modern psychologist would call 'wish-fulfilment'! Take the opening portrait of Tricotrin, set in the most gorgeous wine-harvest scenery you can imagine, add 'the women-faces its tranquil pools had mirrored', and remember 'the sun breaking through the foliage above in manifold gleams and glories that touched the turning leaves bright red as fire':

> It was a beautiful homeric head; bold, kingly, careless, noble, with the royalty of the lion in its gallant poise, and the challenge of the eagle in its upward gesture; the head which an artist would have given to his Hector, or his Phoebus, or his God Lycœus. The features were beautiful too, in their varied and eloquent meanings; with their poet's brows, their reveller's laugh, their soldier's daring, their student's thought, their many and conflicting utterances, whose contradictions made one unity— the unity of genius.

If we already know what an Ouida hero is like, we are not surprised to learn immediately that he had the genius of a Mozart (he possessed a 'Straduarius'), the eloquence of a Mirabeau, the sagacity of a Talleyrand, and that, had he wished, he could have been the most famous painter of his age, as indeed he was the foremost. Naturally—one says 'naturally' when one is steeped deep enough in the atmosphere—he was an English peer who had nobly given up his heritage, and, as naturally, was capable of muscular feats which any athlete would envy. They are all like that, her heroes, except that they are usually more languid: their lily hands can strangle lions, their unutterable boredom is relieved only by deeds of heroism in battle, their taste, and often their performance, in the arts is beyond reproach. And the spirit does not belie the body, as a rule: the endurance of these men, their self-control (exceptionally broken down by wild passion), their loyalty, their untarnishable honour, prove that they are no mere whited sepulchres; often they are men of staggering ability. The wicked, of course, are unspeakably vile.

Her women, alas, are rarely so perfect; outside, yes, they are so overwhelmingly lovely that princes fawn at their feet, statesmen throw away their careers for a kiss, lesser mortals dare death for the dimple of a smile. But inside—ah!—cruel, cunning, cold (Ouida's style is infectious), without hearts: filled only with social ambition and the love of feminine power, they are demons who batten on revenge, as described by this great castigator of her sex. Not that all, by any means, are like that. The Princess Souroff is as spotless as any of Ouida's heroes; the girl in *The Massarenes* is as honest a piece of womanhood as you would meet anywhere. But the picture in the main is flattering to males, and for that reason men would read the novels; and women might perhaps read them to meet in them the perfect man. And moreover, there is Cigarette, the *vivandière* of *Under Two Flags*, to appeal to both sexes, the charmingly romantic loyal heroine, who met her death because she loved too well, and whom only the sternest would blame because she had loved too often.

There already, perhaps, are enough elements to give popularity, but to that you must add Ouida's immense variety of personages and scenes. Her heroes can be statesmen, guardsmen, Bohemians, singers, King's Messengers: her women can be real or sham noble, or poverty-stricken peasants, or gypsy fortune-tellers; because she deals in extremes she rarely touches on the middle classes. Her scenes take us roaming all over Europe and some of Africa, and besides, within the geography, what places! Palaces, hovels, haunts of virtue or vice high or low, courts and galleys, wild woodlands, suffocating deserts, mountains or coasts; and who dare say that her descriptions of interiors or exteriors are not vivid, even if wordy, and do not give the mind other places to dwell in, abundantly, lavishly (these epithets recur), for the reader's ease, satisfaction, or excitement? And then, on the whole, she manages the story so well; we are all agog to know what is going to happen next; it is difficult even now to put one of her books down. We shall skip, no doubt, run our eye swiftly down the page, refuse, perhaps unwisely, the trimmings of the ample dish. Usually her books are well constructed, though it has happened to me to read *Moths*, omitting the middle third, without finding that it mattered much. This will not do, however, with most of her books. There is, indeed, too much detail, repetition even; but the truth is that she was in love with life, and though it may be easy to make fun of her art, at least it makes us also in love with life, even with her fantastic vision of it. And since we ourselves are thrall to her, how shall we be surprised that the Victorians fell easy victims?

And then there are two aspects which we can well imagine more attractive to the Victorians than to us: the first is the characters themselves, the second what they imply. We do not today care so much for types, we prefer the analysis of a personality, and Ouida's persons are types, or rather, they are what used to be called 'humours'; they represent qualities, such as good or evil, heroism or vileness, courage, cruelty and so on; and, here is the appeal, when she depicts good qualities, physical or moral, they are those which most of us, at some time of our lives, if generally in very early youth, wish to acquire. And, believing in her heroes so thoroughly as she does, we believe in them too, at least while we read her, and it is probable that the Victorians, simpler-minded that we are, believed in them more easily than we can. There then were the people one would give anything to be, and, since one believed in them, one could identify one's self with them for the moment. What more rapturous experience could there be?

And it is again because we are not so simple-minded as the Victorians (apparently) were—we have become horridly adult, what our forebears would call cynical—that we probably cannot so whole-heartedly enjoy the other aspect, her moral vision. She had values; her novels were, at least, about something, and those values were, undoubtedly, right, though many would today call them sentimental; but not the thousands who cherish *Beau Geste*. She was all for honesty, loyalty, self-sacrifice, stoic endurance, not from a sense of duty, but—and here the Victorians spied the serpent—from love. And above all she admired generosity, generosity of life, in living, in giving of self. Her hatred of injustice showed itself especially in her stories of Italian peasant life, and it is not for nothing that the memorial erected at her birthplace, Bury St. Edmunds, is flanked by statuettes labelled 'Sympathy' and 'Generosity'. She was all whips and scorpions for those who sacrifice the profounder emotions to the tinsel of fashion or success; she hated all meanness, all self-seeking. Her novels are in a way nonsense, yes; the whole thing is far too highly-coloured, flaunting, improbable, not to say impossible; everything is at an unattainable pitch, but the materials are the right ones, if not for truth as we have come to see it, at least for a flamboyant beauty. In reading her it is not possible to think of her as anything but popular: she gives life and its glamour with both hands. Her work is always over-full, her language often incorrect, her excursions into foreign tongues, dead and living, sometimes unfortunate. Her work will not stand the test of actuality, but it will stand that of an undisciplined imaginative truth. Of course she was read, of course she was loved; and it would not be surprising if a new cheap edition of *Under Two Flags* should sell its thousands. Other books of hers no doubt require a more recondite taste, the taste that is content to abide a mass of flummery for the sake of a few pearls, the taste that can see virtue in abundance, even if it is over-abundance. 'Her every page', Mr. Beerbohm remarks, 'is a riot of unpolished epigrams and unpolished poetry of vision': and those qualities were more appreciated in her day than they are now. Most significant, however, is the fact that Mr. Beerbohm dedicated *More* 'To Mlle. de la Ramée, with the author's compliments, and to Ouida with his love'. That, perhaps, in the final explanation of her popularity.